THE
WORLD CRISIS
1916-1918

VOLUME II

BY
THE RT. HON. WINSTON S. CHURCHILL,
C.H., M.P.

NEW YORK
CHARLES SCRIBNER'S SONS
1927

CONTENTS

TABLE OF MAPS, CHARTS, ETC.

THE WORLD CRISIS
1916–1918

CHAPTER XII

AT THE MINISTRY OF MUNITIONS

I rejoin the Government—Munitions Supply—The Admiralty Claims—
The Limiting Factors—Reorganisation of the Ministry of Munitions
—The Munitions Council—The Work of the Munitions Council—
Sir James Stevenson—My Memo. of November 9, 1916—The Attack
by Armoured Vehicles—Scale and Intensity—Futility of Pure
Attrition—Six Forms of War Machinery—Blasting Power and
Moving Power—The Fateful Issue.

ON July 16, 1917, the Prime Minister invited me to join
the new Government. He proposed to me either the
Ministry of Munitions or the newly created Air Ministry,
with the proviso that if I chose the latter, he must have till
the afternoon to make certain personal rearrangements in the
Administration. I said at once that I preferred Munitions;
and the matter was settled in as many words as I here set
down.

The appointment was announced the next morning. There
was an outcry among those who at that time had accustomed
themselves to regard me with hostility. An immediate pro-
test was made by the Committee of the National Union of
Conservative Associations, and an influential deputation of
Unionist Members presented themselves to the leader of the
Party in strong complaint. Mr. Lloyd George had however
prepared the ground with his accustomed patience. Lord
Northcliffe was on a mission to the United States, and ap-
peased. Sir Edward Carson and General Smuts were warm
advocates. The group of Ministers who had successfully
prevented my entering the Government on its formation was
no longer intact. Some had been previously placated: the
remnant acquiesced. And Mr. Bonar Law, who had always

been a friend, returned a very stiff answer to his deputation. I was re-elected for Dundee by a remarkable majority, and took up my duties without delay. Not allowed to make the plans, I was set to make the weapons.

The internal conditions of munitions supply, and indeed the whole structure of the British Executive, were vastly different from those I had quitted twenty months before, and still more from the days when I was First Lord of the Admiralty. In the first period of the war—indeed almost to the end of 1915—the resources of Britain far exceeded any organisation which could employ them. Whatever was needed for the fleets and armies had only to be ordered in good time and on a large enough scale. The chief difficulty was to stretch the mind to a hitherto unimagined size of events. Megalomania was a positive virtue. Indeed, to add a nought, or a couple of noughts, to almost any requisition or plan for producing war supplies would have constituted an act of merit. Now all was changed. Three years of the struggle had engaged very nearly the whole might of the nation. Munition production of every kind was already upon a gigantic scale. The whole island was an arsenal. The enormous national factories which Mr. Lloyd George had planned were just beginning to function. The first difficulties with the Trade Unions about the dilution of labour had been over-come. Hundreds of thousands of women were making shells and fuses cheaper and better than the most skilled craftsmen had done before the war. The keenest spirits in British industry were gathered as State servants in the range of palatial hotels which housed the Ministry of Munitions. The former trickles and streamlets of war supplies now flowed in rivers rising continuously.

Nevertheless the demands of the fighting fronts eagerly and easily engulfed all that could be produced. We were in the presence of requirements at once imperative and apparently insatiable; and now at last our ultimate capacity

began to come into view. I found myself in a world of 'Limiting Factors' and 'Priorities.' All problems were complicated by the fact that the Admiralty had not been brought within the general sphere of munitions supply. When the munitions crisis of May, 1915, had overwhelmed the War Office and the Liberal Government, the Admiralty had not been found wanting in any important respect. All supplies for the Fleets were at hand or coming forward in abundance in consequence of the orders we had placed at the beginning of the war, and which had received a further expansion during my partnership with Lord Fisher. The Admiralty therefore had been able to retain their separate and privileged position. They had their own great supply departments, their own factories, their own programmes, and their own allegiances. In a period when a general view and a just proportion were the master-keys, they vigorously asserted their claim to be a realm within a realm—efficient, colossal, indispensable, well-disposed, but independent.

In their view the Navy came first not only in essentials, but in refinements, not only in minima but in precautionary margins. And of all these the Board of Admiralty was the sole judge. Theirs was the first claim upon materials and skilled labour of all kinds. After that had been met, they were genuinely glad that the Armies, the Air Force and, at a considerable interval, the civil population should be adequately maintained. This dominating position was fortified by the grave anxieties of the U-boat campaign, and lost nothing from the virile personality of the new First Lord.

The career of Sir Eric Geddes during the war had been astonishing. As the General Manager of an important Railway, versed in every detail of its working from the humblest to the highest, he possessed not only the practical organising power of a skilful business man, but the *quasi*-official outlook of the head of a great public service. To this he added those qualities of mental and physical energy, of industry, of thoroughness and compulsive force, often successful, always admirable, and never more needed than at this time. He had risen rapidly under Mr. Lloyd George to be one of the principal figures of the Ministry of Munitions in its early days. He had reorganised the railways of the British front in France with the rank and uniform of a Major-General. He had controlled the Supply Departments of the Navy with the rank and uniform of a Vice-Admiral. Now the same hand which had conducted him through these swift and surprising transformations placed him at the head of the Board of Admiralty. He reinforced its particularism with an ability and domineering vigour all his own.

Judged by the truest sense of proportion, the Navy had a right to absolute priority in all that was necessary to grapple with the supreme peril of the U-boat attack, including the vast replacement of the sunken merchant ships. But when such rights were extended to all the other branches of the Naval Service, and even to strengthening the Battle Fleet and increasing its already overflowing resources of stores, guns and ammunition, a serious inroad was made upon what was due to the armies and to the ever-growing service of the air. The War Cabinet, riveted by the U-boat attack and rightly determined to give the Navy all it wanted for the purpose of meeting it, was not found capable of drawing the necessary distinction between this and less imperious services. In consequence the Grand Fleet absorbed in the final phases of the war a larger share of our resources than was its due, and our war effort in the field was unwarrantably diminished to that extent.

The principal limiting factors to munitions production with which I was confronted in the autumn of 1917 were four in number, viz. shipping (tonnage), steel, skilled labour and dollars. The last of these had been rendered less acute by the accession of the United States to the Allies. We had already sold a thousand millions sterling of American securities, and had borrowed heavily to feed and equip ourselves, and our Allies, before this decisive event. Our transatlantic credits were practically exhausted at the beginning of 1917. The dollar situation was now somewhat relieved. A door that would otherwise have closed altogether was now held partially open. None the less the limits of the power of purchase both in American and Canadian dollars imposed a restrictive finger on the layout of every programme.

The stringency in shipping was acute. The losses of the U-boat war, the requirements of the armies in every theatre, the food and what remained of the trade of Britain, the needs of the Allies, the increasing desires of the United States, and the importations of all the raw materials of war, had drawn out our Mercantile Marine to its most intense strain. Tonnage therefore was at this period the controlling factor in our production. Steel ranked next to tonnage, and was a more direct measure of war effort. The steel output of Great Britain had already nearly doubled. Mines which would not pay in peace had come into active production. But in the main we depended for iron ore upon the north coast of Spain, and all vessels which carried it ran perilous voyages amid frequent sinkings. In addition we bought finished steel to the utmost limit of our dollars from the United States and Canada, as well as shell castings of every intermediate form.

Of all we produced or obtained the Admiralty took their fill. The prime need was the replacement of merchant ships sunk by submarines. The War Cabinet had approved an ambitious programme of building 3,000,000 tons of mercantile shipping in 1918. This claimed priority even over the innumerable anti-U-boat flotillas. Next came the improved heavy-shell outfits which the disappointing experiences of Jutland were claimed to require. Not till these and other less vital naval demands had been satisfied could the requirements of the British armies for guns, shells, tanks and indispensable subsidiaries be considered. We had also to provide a large proportion of steel for the French shell factories under arrangements we had made early in the war: and to Italy we had to send both steel and coal in serious quantities under agreements, failure in which would have crippled her fighting strength.

Lastly, there were the limits fixed by the supply of skilled labour. And here again the Army and the Air Force clashed with the Admiralty at a hundred points. All the most perfect lethal instruments were demanded at once by the three Services, and at the same time ever-increasing numbers of skilled artisans were drawn into the fighting sphere. The ceaseless process of training and dilution steadily expanded our supply. But in spite of the earnest help afforded by all the responsible Labour leaders, Trade Union principles and prejudices made every step delicate. Such were the main features of the task with which I had the honour to be entrusted.

If I were to attempt to exhaust the details, this chapter would become a volume. We depended, and through us the Allies, upon the sea power which drew from the remotest portions of the globe not only the bulky imports, but all those rare and scarce commodities without which steel cannot be hardened or explosives made, or Science realize its full death-dealing power, or an island people get their daily bread. Some of these aspects will emerge in the narrative.

The growth of the Ministry of Munitions had far outstripped its organisation. A year had passed since its creator, Mr. Lloyd George, had moved on to still more intense spheres. The two gifted Ministers who had succeeded him, Mr. Montagu and Dr. Addison, had dealt with the needs as they arose, shouldering one responsibility after another, adding department to department and branch to branch, without altering in essentials the central organisation from the form it had assumed in the empirical and convulsive period of creation. All the main and numberless minor decisions still centred upon the Minister himself. I found a staff of 12,000 officials organised in no less than fifty principal departments each claiming direct access to the Chief, and requiring a swift flow of decisions upon most intricate and inter-related problems. I set to work at once to divide and distribute this dangerous concentration of power.

Under a new system the fifty departments of the Ministry were grouped into ten large units each in charge of a head who was directly responsible to the Minister. These ten heads of groups of departments were themselves formed into a Council like a Cabinet. The Members of the Council were charged with dual functions: first, to manage their group of departments; secondly, to take a general interest in the whole business of the Ministry. They were to develop a 'Council sense,' and not to regard themselves as confined to their own special sphere. Each group of departments was denoted by a letter. Thus D was design, G guns, F finance, P projectiles, X explosives, and so on. By ringing the changes upon these letters committees could be formed exactly adapted to handle any particular topic, while the general movement of business was held firmly together by means of a co-ordinating or 'Clamping' committee. The 'big business men' who now formed the Council were assisted by a strong cadre of Civil Servants, and I obtained for this purpose from the Admiralty my old friends Sir William Graham Greene and Mr. Masterton-Smith. Thus we had at once the initiative, drive, force and practical experience of the open competitive world coupled with those high standards of experience, of official routine, and of method, which are the qualifications of the Civil Service.

The new organisation was announced to the public on August 18 in a memorandum from which the following paragraphs are taken:—

'. . . In the fourth year of the war, we are no longer tapping the stored-up resources of national industry or mobilising them and applying them for the first time to war. The magnitude of the effort and of the achievement approximates continually to the limits of possibility. Already in many directions the frontiers are in sight. It is therefore necessary not simply to expand, but to go back over ground already covered, and by more economical processes, by closer organisation, and by thrifty and harmonious methods, to glean and gather a further reinforcement of war power.

'It is necessary for this purpose that the Minister of Munitions should be aided and advised by a Council formally established. The time has come to interpose between more than fifty separate departments on the one hand and the Minister on the other, an organism which in the main will play a similar part and serve similar needs as the Board of Admiralty or the Army Council. It has been decided therefore to form the departments of the Ministry into ten groups, classified as far as possible by kindred conditions, placing in superintendence over each group an experienced officer of the Ministry, and to form these officers into a Council for the transaction of business of all kinds in accordance with the general policy which the Minister receives from the Cabinet.'[1]

Here is my Council as it began:

Financial Secretary.—Sir Laming Worthington-Evans.
Parliamentary Secretary.—Mr. Kellaway.

Groups of Departments

F. *Finance.*—Sir Herbert Hambling.
D. *Design.*—Major-General Bingham.
S. *Steel and Iron.*—Mr. John Hunter.
M. *Materials.*—Sir Ernest Moir.
X. *Explosives.*— Sir Keith Price.
P. *Projectiles, etc.*—Sir James Stevenson.
G. *Guns.*—Sir Glynn West.
E. *Engines.*—Sir Arthur Duckham.
A. *Allies.*—Sir Frederick Black, later Sir Charles Ellis.
L. *Labour.*—Sir Stephenson Kent.

The Secretariat (*at a later date*)

R. *Requirements and Statistics.*—Mr. Layton.
War Office Representative.—Major-General Furse.
W. *Trench Warfare and Inventions.*—Major-General Seely.

[1] *See* Appendix.

The relief was instantaneous. I was no longer oppressed by heaps of bulky files. Every one of my ten Councillors was able to give important final decisions in his own sphere. The daily Council meeting kept them in close relation with each other and with the general scheme; while the system of committees of councillors enabled special questions to be brought to speedy conclusion. Once the whole organisation was in motion it never required change. Instead of struggling through the jungle on foot I rode comfortably on an elephant whose trunk could pick up a pin or uproot a tree with equal ease, and from whose back a wide scene lay open.[1]

I confined myself to the assignment and regulation of work, to determining the emphasis and priority of particular supplies, to the comprehensive view of the war programmes, and to the initiation of special enterprises. After five months' experience of the new system I was able to say, 'I practically always approve a Council Committee report exactly as it comes. I think I have hardly ever altered a word. I read each report through with great attention and see the decision on the question, which I know is ever so much better than I could have produced myself, if I had studied it for two whole days.'

At the Ministry of Munitions I worked with incomparably the largest and most powerful staff in my experience. Here were gathered the finest business brains of the country working with might and main and with disinterested loyalty for the common cause. Many if not most of the leading men stood at the head of those industries which were most expanded by war needs. They therefore resigned altogether the immense fortunes which must inevitably have come to them, had they continued as private contractors. They served the State for

---

[1] My minutes and memoranda of the time tell the story much better than any subsequent account which I could write. Accordingly from very large numbers I have selected enough to give a picture alike of the problem and of the movement of events. These will be found in an Appendix.

honour alone. They were content to see men of lesser standing
in their own industries amass great wealth and extend the scale
of their business. In the service of the Crown there was a keen
rivalry among them; and the position of Member of Council
with its general outlook was deeply prized. According to the
Statute constituting the office, the whole authority rested with
the Minister; but in practice the Council had a true collective
responsibility.

If in these pages I dwell with pride upon the extraordinary
achievements of the Munitions Council in the field of supply,
it is not to appropriate the credit. That belongs in the first
instance to Mr. Lloyd George, who gathered together the
great majority of these able men, and whose foresight in
creating the national factories laid the foundations for subsequent production. It belongs also to the men who did the
work, who quarried and shaped the stones, and to whose
faithful, resourceful, untiring contrivance and exertion the
Army and the nation owe a lasting debt.

It would be difficult and invidious for me to single out
individuals among those who are still living. Their services
have not been unrewarded by the Crown. But there is one
who has gone from us to whom this account offers me the opportunity of paying tribute.

James Stevenson[1] was the most ingenious and compulsive
manager and masterer of difficulties—material or personal—
with whom I have ever served. Whether at the Ministry of
Munitions or after the war when he accompanied me to the
War Office and to the Colonial Office, no task however
laborious, no problem however baffling, once it had been
remitted to him, was ever a source of subsequent difficulty or
complaint. With him, with his close colleague, Sir Arthur
Duckham, and with the young profound Professor Layton,
who assembled and presented the weekly statistics, I was
brought into the closest daily contact. These three con-

[1] Afterwards Lord Stevenson.

stituted for me the mainspring, both of action and of review, by which the central control of the immense organisation was exercised. Stevenson is dead. He died at fifty, worn out, as thoroughly as a brave soldier in the trenches, by his exertions in the public service. He left behind him a reputation, sustained by the opinion of Ministers of many Departments and of all Parties, for ability, integrity and devotion which should afford an example and an inspiration to the business men of Britain. To the deep appreciation of his work and gifts declared by those in a position to judge, I wish to add my testimony.

*   *   *   *   *

The relief afforded by the new organisation in the general business of supply, gave me time to pursue my ideas upon mechanical attack. After the apparition of the tanks at the taking of Flers a year earlier, in September, 1916, and in the disappointment with which the end of the Somme battle oppressed the Cabinet, I had, though in nominal opposition, some credit in official circles. At the wish of the Minister of Munitions I had written a paper upon 'The greater application of mechanical power to the prosecution of an offensive on land.' Mr. Montagu had it printed for the Committee of Imperial Defence and circulated it to the Cabinet.

November 9, 1916.

1. The conditions of this war deny to the stronger power, whether on sea or land, its legitimate offensive scope. In all previous wars the stronger army was able to force matters to a final decision. The great developments of defensive power now prevent this.

2. We shall never have a superiority in numbers sufficient to triumph by itself. At present the fighting forces are much too evenly balanced. We have perhaps a superiority of five to four in fighting formations on all fronts, but the enemy's advantage of being on interior lines more than covers this. Even if we have a superiority of six to four, that will be insufficient, and we are not likely to see a greater superiority than this for a very long time.

3. Frontal attacks were abandoned forty years ago on account of the severity of fire. Now that the severity of fire has enormously increased and is constantly increasing, they are forced upon us in the absence of flanks.

4. Two methods of frontal attack have been tried. First the unlimited, as at Loos and Champagne, where the troops were given a distant objective behind the enemy's lines and told to march on that; and second, the limited form as tried by the Germans at Verdun, and by ourselves and the French on the Somme. Neither produces decisive results. The unlimited simply leads to the troops being brought up against uncut wire and undamaged machine guns. The limited always enables the enemy to move his artillery away, and to sell a very little ground at a heavy price in life, gaining time all the while to construct new defences in the rear.

.   .   .   .   .

8. An attack depends on two processes—

    (*a*) Blasting power and
    (*b*) Moving power;

blasting power is very well provided for in the constantly improving supplies of guns and shells, but moving power is in its infancy.

9. Two things stop the offensive movement of armies—

    (*a*) Bullets and fragments of shell which destroy the motive power of men, and
    (*b*) The confusion of the conflict.

.   .   .   .   .

15. A method of overcoming these difficulties exists. It may be shortly described as 'the attack by armoured vehicles.' I cannot pretend to do more than outline it and suggest it. I am not an inventor or designer. I have no means of testing and elaborating these ideas. Evidently they require study, experiment, and at least six months' preparation.

But now is the time in the winter to organise and perfect this method of attack. The 'Tanks' have shown the way. But they are only a beginning.[1]

[1] The full text of this Memorandum is printed in the Appendix.

A year had passed. Nothing had been done. Mr. Asquith's Government had fallen, Mr. Montagu was at the India Office and I had succeeded his successor at the Ministry of Munitions. I had therefore the chance and the duty of giving effect in one form or another to the project of a mechanical battle which I had advocated when a private member.

In the interval the tanks had been consistently misused by the generals, and their first prestige was markedly diminished. The War Office and General Headquarters had demanded from the Ministry of Munitions guns and shells on the basis of a thirty weeks' continuous British offensive in 1918. The sketch programmes which I found upon taking office were all framed on this assumption. No one contemplated such an event as a German offensive. The only question open was what was the best method of attacking the enemy. I drew up the following paper in the light of these acceptances.[1]

To the War Cabinet.

October 21, 1917.

1. In deciding upon the Munitions Programme for 1918, the first question to be answered is, 'What is the War Plan? When is it to reach its climax? Have we the possibility of winning in 1918, and if so, how are we going to do it?. . .'

2. It is obvious that the defeat and breaking-up of the German armies in the West affords the best, the simplest and the swiftest method of arriving at decisive victory. The only question is, 'Have we the power to do it?' It would be a thousand pities to discard this direct and obvious method of victory in favour of weaker, more roundabout, protracted and far less decisive strategy, unless we are convinced that we have not the power to conquer on the Western Front. . . .

3. Ever since the autumn of 1914 we have heard the same accounts of the exhaustion of the enemy's man-power, of the decline of his morale, and of how near we stand, if we only make the effort, to the supreme and final result. Every year we have in consequence made exertions on the greatest possible

---

[1] The omitted paragraphs from this paper will be found in the Appendix. See p. 303.

scale, and every year the close of the campaign has seen the
enemy's front, however dinted, yet unbroken. But this in
itself is by no means conclusive; for the effects of our efforts
upon the enemy have been cumulative, the exhaustion of his
man-power and the deterioration of his morale have been
progressive; our superiority in munitions of all kinds has
continually augmented; the offensive power of the British
Army has continually increased; that of the French is still
formidable. The German armies in the West, on the other
hand, appear to have completely lost their offensive power.
The Germans have now been for four campaigns extended to
their maximum war effort. They have maintained in continual battle upon all fronts armies of four or five millions of
men. The very efficiency of their organisation enabled them
to strain themselves to their fullest compass from the outset,
and the draft which they have made upon the life-energies
of their whole nation is proportionately equal to and possibly
greater than the draft which has been made upon the life-
energies of France. We can measure the effect of the strain
upon the French; and this affords perhaps the best guide to
the actual remaining fighting power of Germany. Therefore
it may well be that conclusions drawn from our disappoint-
ments in four successive campaigns would not apply to the
fifth, and that the assertions and hopes that have proved
unjustified in four successive campaigns might be vindicated
in the end. For this reason it is imperative not to abandon the
Western effort, and resign ourselves to the formidable dangers
involved in the prolongation of the war into 1919, without the
most searching consideration of all our resources.

4. If we are to conquer in the West, we must for that purpose
provide for the concentration of all our methods of attack
upon the enemy simultaneously at the decisive period. . . .

5. Success can only be achieved by the *scale and intensity*
of our offensive effort within a limited period. We are seeking
to conquer the enemy's army and not his position; and one
stroke must follow another so rapidly that no breathing space
for recovery or recuperation is afforded. Unless the effort
reaches and is maintained at the required degree of *intensity*
or on a sufficiently large scale, the campaign will be indecisive
like all the others, however successful and profitable individual
battles may have been. It is this principle of the intensity

of the effort during a culminating period which must govern all our calculations. With armies so large as those which confront each other in the West, and with numerical superiority on our side which cannot be large, and may well be non-existent, a succession of heavy blows at intervals during the campaigning season may, however successful, result only in reciprocal losses without substantially altering the strategic situation. A policy of pure attrition between armies so evenly balanced cannot lead to a decision. It is not a question of wearing down the enemy's reserves, but of wearing them down so rapidly that recovery and replacement of shattered divisions is impossible. In a struggle between, say, 250 divisions on one side and 200 on the other, the small margin of superiority possessed by the stronger cannot be made to tell decisively before the winter respite is reached unless the war effort of the offensive reaches a far higher degree of general intensity than has hitherto been found possible. In other words, our attack must be of such a character that a division once used up *on either side* cannot reach the battle-front again during the culminating period in time to influence the conclusion. Unless this problem can be solved satisfactorily, we shall simply be wearing each other out on a gigantic scale and with fearful sacrifices, without ever reaping the reward.

6. It is clear that in 1918 we cannot hope for any large numerical superiority in men. The relief which will be afforded . . . to the German armies in the West by the collapse of Russia must be set against the reinforcement we shall receive from the United States. I have witnessed with profound disappointment the slow and frugal development of American fighting strength in France. From the day when America entered the war, the stream of American manhood, trained, half-trained, or untrained, to Europe should have been continuous, and all the available means of transportation should have been assembled and continually used to their utmost capacity—the men, of course, being properly trained either on one side of the Atlantic or the other. The melancholy decision to adopt a different form of armament, both for the infantry and artillery, has also seriously retarded the development of American war power. This is now being realized by the American authorities, but too late. We cannot therefore count on any great superiority in numbers on the

Western Front in 1918. Our calculations must proceed upon an assumption that there will be no decisive preponderance in the number of formed divisions or in the number of men in the line or in the reserves available within the year. We are however entitled to count upon a marked and possibly increasing superiority in quality and morale. There remain in addition only the great province of war machinery and the resources of superior generalship operating through war machinery. Will these suffice?

7. There are six principal forms of machinery by which our infantry on the Western Front (slightly superior in numbers, markedly superior in quality) may be aided, viz.:

> Artillery preponderance,
> Air supremacy,
> Railway or mechanical mobility,
> Trench-mortar development,
> Tank development,
> Gas development.

In what way can these be combined and applied by generalship so as to produce the maximum intensity of offensive power during the culminating period? . . .

V.

25. It should not be supposed that victory in the West depends indispensably on a large superiority in numbers. When one army, partly from superiority in numbers, partly from superiority in morale, feels itself decidedly the stronger, it seeks to assume the offensive. What is lacking is an effective method of the offensive. A very large superiority in numbers would of course be one way, but we have no prospect of getting this. Three or four times the artillery we have at present would be another method; but there is no prospect of getting this in the immediate future. Still, if a means could be found whereby the stronger and better army could advance continuously *and at a sufficient speed* on a front of twenty or thirty miles, a general retirement would unquestionably be forced upon the German armies.

26. How then are we to find this method of continuous offensive, which is the inherent right of the stronger and better army, and the absence of which is the sole cause of the pro-

longation of the war? We have at present only the artillery.
If you concentrate the bulk of the artillery of a great nation
on a narrow battle-front and feed it with the whole industry
of the people, it is possible to pound and pulverize certain
areas of ground, so that a limited advance can certainly be
made. But the artillery is so local in its action, so costly in
its use, and so ponderous in its movement that the rate of the
advance has not hitherto led to any decisive strategic results.
It is clear therefore that the artillery alone is not sufficient,
and will never be sufficient, to impart to the stronger army
the certain and irresistible means of advancing which it
requires. It is becoming apparent that the 'blasting power'
of the artillery is only one of the factors required for a satisfactory method of the offensive. 'Moving power' must be
developed equally with 'blasting power.' 'Moving power'
deserves as sustained a study, as extensive an application,
and as large a share of our resources as have hitherto been
given to the 'blasting power' of the artillery.

'Moving power,' in the shape of railways, motor transport,
light railways and tramways, has already attained large
dimensions up to the edge of the battlefield; but 'moving
power' *on the battlefield itself* is practically limited to the arms
and legs of human beings. This is not enough, and it never
will be enough, and until it can be supplemented *on the
battlefield* by machinery of one kind or another which can be
brought into being and kept in working order in spite of
intense battle conditions, the stronger army will remain
robbed of its method of advance.

29. If we may assume a stronger and better army equally
equipped with 'blasting power' and 'moving power,' and
capable of operating continuously on a front sufficiently
broad, its success would not necessarily be dependent upon
the relative numbers of troops available on either side in the
whole theatre of war. Whatever his strength in other parts,
the enemy would be under a continual imperative obligation
of arresting this offensive movement on a given front. Some-
one must stop the tiger. If the rate of advance was sufficiently
rapid, lack of a great superiority in numbers would not
paralyse the attackers; and even bringing superior numbers to
the spot would not help the defenders. For the defensive,
even more than for the offensive, the numbers of men which

can be usefully employed in given areas of ground is severely limited. Just as it may be said that the 'intensity' of the offensive all along the front should be such as to make the whole line rock and keep the enemy in continual movement and uncertainty, so the rate of progress of the attack on the main battlefield and the obstruction of communications behind it should be sufficient to prevent reinforcement before essential points are lost.

30. When we see these great armies in the West spread out in thin lines hundreds of miles long and organised in depth only at very few points, it is impossible to doubt that if one side discovered, developed, and perfected a definite method of advancing continuously, albeit upon a fairly limited front, a decisive defeat would be inflicted upon the other. If therefore we could by organised mechanical processes and equipment impart this faculty to our armies in 1918 or in 1919, it would be an effective substitute for a great numerical preponderance in numbers. What other substitute can we look for? Where else is our superiority coming from?

31. A survey of these mechanical possibilities together with a computation of our resources compared to those of the enemy should afford the best means of judging the fateful question already postulated, viz., whether we have the means of overthrowing finally the enemy's main armies on the Western Front during the campaign of 1918. . . .

CHAPTER XIII

THE MUNITIONS BUDGET

Competing Needs and Rival Authorities—The Priorities Committee—
Resources and Demands—Duplication and Waste of Effort—Over-
insurance—Memorandum on the Munitions Budget—Tonnage:
Iron Ore—Allocation of Steel—Distribution of Labour—Explosives
—Chemical Warfare—Guns and Ammunition—The Rival Artilleries
on the Western Front—Aeroplanes; Tanks; Dollars—Summary
of Recommendations—Ship Plates and the Tank Programme—
An Unexpected Cut in Tonnage—Efforts to Retrieve the Loss—
Letter to the Shipping Controller—Pressure on the French—Re-
casting the Programme—A Note to the War Cabinet—All ends well.

BY the middle of October the Munitions Council had
completed a comprehensive study of the whole of our
material resources to which I had directed their efforts. I was
therefore able to frame the Munitions Budget for the coming
year. The difficulties of this task far exceeded those of the
budgets for which Chancellors of the Exchequer are usually
responsible. The enormous variety of needs for which provision must be made could be surmounted by systematised
collective study. But the fierce rivalry of so many authorities,
and the dependence of our programmes upon the decisions
of others, made the work complicated and baffling in the last
degree.

In one quarter of our horizon stood the Shipping Controller,
Sir Joseph Maclay, a most able Glasgow shipowner with deep
knowledge, a charming personality and the unbounded confidence of Mr. Bonar Law. He estimated the maximum
tonnage available for all purposes; and his figures, framed in a
conservative and Caledonian spirit, were accepted by the
War Cabinet. In another quarter stood the Chancellor of
the Exchequer, Mr. Bonar Law, one of the all-powerful

Triumvirate. He also took, as was his duty, an extremely restrained view of the limits of dollar credits, both in the United States and Canada. To anything we could buy in Britain the Treasury interposed no obstacle; but we could not realise our programmes unless we were able to make very large purchases of steel from the United States, of unfilled shells from Canada and of nitrates from Chili. Thirdly, there arose the Minister of National Service, Sir Auckland Geddes, whose duty it was—outside a large field over which the Ministry of Munitions reigned—to apportion all the available man-power and to provide the recruits for the fighting services. Last, and not least of all, loomed the portentous figure of Sir Eric Geddes, First Lord of the Admiralty, charged with the paramount duties of maintaining the Fleet, of crushing the U-boats and of rebuilding the Mercantile Marine. For these purposes the Admiralty was armed not only with Absolute Priority, but possessed a monopoly control over all the firms with which they were accustomed to deal. This priority was interpreted so harshly that skilled men had to be found on one occasion for potato-peeling machines for the Grand Fleet, while they were actually being withdrawn from making range-finders for the anti-aircraft guns.[1]

The attitude of the War Office and the Air Ministry towards us was somewhat different. They lived by our supplies, and to that extent were on our side. They not only demanded the supplies on an ever-increasing scale, but they also simultaneously demanded as recruits for the fighting forces the workmen, skilled and unskilled, without which these supplies could not be produced. Against all these potentates the Ministry of Munitions sallied out to do battle. Over everybody sate, as was proper, the War Cabinet, a final court of appeal. But the business of the court was heavily congested, and neither its time nor its temper was unlimited. There was therefore set up in the autumn of 1917 the 'Priorities Com-

[1] This was of course corrected when discovered.

mittee,' presided over by General Smuts. On this the Departments fought and tore for every ton of steel and freight. Never, I suspect, in all the vicissitudes of his career has General Smuts stood more in need of those qualities of tact and adroitness for which among his many virtues he is renowned.

One of my difficulties was in having to argue on so many fronts at once. Facts and reasoning used in one direction for one purpose could be quoted in resistance to another. Because I had thought it right on a general view of the situation to urge that strong efforts should be made to re-equip the Italian armies after Caporetto, I was forever confronted with the argument, 'If you can spare all that for the Italians, you cannot be so badly off yourself.' Or again, in the fight to secure a handful of steel plates for the tank programme, we encountered at first the odious statement: 'But the Army doesn't want any more; General Headquarters does not rank them very high in their priorities; they have not done well at Paschendale; they cannot cope with the mud, etc.'

The War Cabinet, and particularly the Prime Minister, always took a great interest in tanks. At the end of the year after the Battle of Cambrai this became accentuated. They recorded the most solemn adjurations upon the importance of tank construction with the utmost speed and in the largest numbers. But at the same time they ruled that the Admiralty demand for ship plates for the Mercantile Marine, which was several hundred times greater than would ever be needed for tanks, should retain their super-priority. Since we were unable to overcome Sir Eric Geddes by reason, it became necessary to gorge him with ship plates. This the Munitions Council and Sir John Hunter's steel department soon succeeded in doing. The Admiralty's merchant shipbuilding programme of three million tons in twelve months proved far beyond even their very great and splendid activities. We watched with unsleeping attention the accumulations which soon began of ship plates in every yard. Not until the moment was ripe did we unmask the guilty fact. The effect was decisive. The proud Department condescended to parley, and eventually the modest requirements of the tank programme were satisfied.

Surveying the whole process in retrospect, I have no doubt it was not—apart from the privileged position of the Admiralty —either unhealthy or inefficient. It would have been better, as I vehemently argued, to assign the whole sphere of man-power to the Ministry of National Service and the whole sphere of material to the Ministry of Munitions, and for the War Cabinet to have adjudicated upon the main distribution. The one great blot upon the high economy of the British war effort in the last year of the struggle was the undue and un-warrantable inroads upon the common fund made by the Admiralty. That they accomplished vital tasks cannot be denied. But when a nation is fighting for its life, the honour lies not in securing the lion's share, but in a just apportionment of limited resources.

DUPLICATION AND WASTE OF EFFORT

To the War Cabinet

November 6, 1917.

IF we are to realise the full war effort of this country in 1918 and in 1919, it is indispensable that the most searching economy of men and material should be practised in every direction and by every Department; that no services should be duplicated; that no more should be taken for any service, however necessary, than is required; and that one central and superior view should regulate every portion of our defensive and offensive system. Unless we are to be con-fronted with a failure in munitions and shipbuilding, and with a very serious diminution in our potential war-making capacity, it is necessary that there should be a general stock-taking.

Those members of the War Cabinet or Government who were members of the Committee of Imperial Defence in the years before the war are of course familiar with every aspect of the 'Invasion' argument. I will therefore content myself with drawing attention to a few simple facts.

During the early months of the war, especially at the beginning, when Germany had the greatest incentive to try to throw a raiding army across the North Sea, we had as our defence against invasion:—

1. The Fleet, with a margin of eight Dreadnoughts.
2. Our submarines and flotillas.
3. Two, and then one, and finally no regular divisions.
4. The Territorial Army, newly mobilised, with hardly any machine guns, with 15-pounder artillery and scarcely any reserves of ammunition, and gunners almost unskilled.
5. No coast fortifications and only a few guns in open batteries at the defended forts.
6. No mine-fields.
7. Practically no aircraft.

In these circumstances the Germans did not choose or did not venture to make an oversea attack.

We now have:—
1. The British Fleet, with a margin of about twenty Dreadnoughts.
2. The American Battle Fleet (the third strongest in the world) if we require it.
3. Enormous mine-fields, covering the German debouches and hampering the movement even of submarine craft.
4. Submarines and flotillas multiplied manifold.
5. The coast-line fortified from end to end with powerful batteries mounted at every port *and still being increased*. Powerful aeroplane forces and a perfect system of coastal watch.
6. A defence scheme devised by Lord French himself, according to the latest experience of this war.
7. A Home Army mostly in its actual battle stations, aggregating a quarter of a million men and supported by a powerful field artillery of upwards of 500 modern guns and howitzers, with boundless supplies of ammunition and enormous numbers of organised mobile or sited machine guns.

8. A million and a quarter other armed and uniformed men behind these.

9. The Volunteers.

Security is no doubt vital, but it must be remembered that if the factor of safety is exaggerated in any one part of our organisation, other parts may be exposed to fatal peril; and that if our strength is dissipated in making sure three or four times over in one direction, we may fail to have the strength available for the general offensive war, and may consequently be compelled impotently to witness the defeat of our Allies one by one.

The very serious situation of the war and the impossibility on present lines of securing any effective numerical superiority or any sufficiently large mechanical superiority over the German armies in the field compel me to bring these aspects of our present arrangements to the notice of the War Cabinet.

*　　*　　*　　*　　*

A few days earlier I had presented the 'Munitions Budget' to the Cabinet. As it covers and explains so many aspects of our war plans and efforts, I reprint it almost in full.

To the War Cabinet.

MUNITIONS BUDGET FOR 1918.

(Provisional.)

November 1, 1917.

1. THE foundation of the Munitions Budget is Tonnage; the ground floor is Steel; and the limiting factor in construction is Labour.

The period covered by this Budget is, broadly speaking, from now to the end of the 1918 offensive, and the figures relate precisely to the twelve months from the 15th November, 1917, to the 15th November, 1918.

2. The following are the principal demands made by the fighting departments upon the Ministry of Munitions for the campaign of 1918 compared with 1917:

(i) The demand of the War Office for the completion of their programme involving a 40 per cent. further increase in the striking power of the artillery, both in guns and ammunition.

(ii) The demand of the Admiralty for doubled shipbuilding materials.

(iii) The demand of the Air Board for tripled aeronautical supplies.

3. *Tonnage.*—The programmes as proposed require the delivery here of 1,100,000 tons per month for munitions alone (*i.e.,* apart from items for other departments included in our tonnage allocation). To secure this there should be assigned to us for all purposes 1,300,000 tons of shipping a month. I propose to place orders abroad somewhat in advance of this figure. If the shipping falls off, the material ordered will be received more slowly. It is better to have a moderate surplus of orders awaiting shipment than not to have the tonnage fully occupied with vitally needed materials.

4. *Iron Ore.*—More than half our total munitions imports consist of iron ore. The blast furnaces could deal with a monthly importation of 735,000 tons of Spanish and Swedish (mainly hematite) ore, and with a monthly home production of 1,500,000 tons of (mainly basic) ore. On the above tonnage basis I count only on getting 635,000 tons of ore, viz.: 550,000 tons from Spain, and 85,000 tons from Sweden. There is a good reserve of Swedish ore, which can be drawn upon in case of need. I estimate that the home production will average over 1,500,000 tons a month.

5. *Steel.*—On this basis we can produce in the year approximately 8,500,000 tons of finished steel product. Orders are being placed for 1,000,000 tons of steel from the United States (included in our tonnage requirements). Arrangements have also been made with the French and with the Shipping Controller to carry approximately 500,000 tons of French Shell Steel already purchased in America which we should otherwise have had to supply from home sources. Having regard to this rearrangement of supplies it may be said that our steel production in relation to our needs and our commitments to the Allies is equivalent to 10,000,000 tons. Out of this every requirement must be met, and if through shipping shrinkage the total production is reduced, all programmes will be affected.

6. *Allocation of Steel.*—Shipbuilding is the first charge on our steel resources. Orders have been given that the rolling mills are to be kept constantly fed to their full and increasing

capacity, and that sections and other shipbuilding components shall be supplied in their proper proportion to the output of plates assigned to the Admiralty, until such time as the ship-yards are provided with material to their full capacity. An agreement has been reached with the Admiralty after a full disclosure of figures whereby a portion of our rolling-mill production, varying from 7,000 to 8,500 tons a week, shall be reserved for all non-Admiralty services (including the War Office and the civilian needs of the country) and the whole of the rest of the production assigned to Admiralty needs. We have already succeeded in raising the Admiralty supply of plates from 16,000 tons a week in July to an average of 20,000 tons a week at the end of September, and subject to their capacity we shall still further raise them gradually up to at least 27,000 tons a week in October, 1918. This with other shipbuilding material to be supplied during the period under forecast is equivalent to a construction of from 2,000,000 to 2,500,000 tons of merchant shipping in addition to warship construction. The twelve months' Admiralty allocation of steel aggregates approximately 2,000,000 tons.

The next principal draft on our Steel Budget is shells. On the programme demanded by the War Office this requires approximately 2,500,000 tons for Great Britain.

The requirements of the Allies for steel of all classes have been cut down to about 700,000 tons in the year, chiefly by the arrangement to ship 500,000 tons of shell steel from the U.S.A. to France. The other direct munition requirements, including aircraft, guns, military railways, tanks, steel-works extensions, &c., are approximately 2,200,000 tons. The War Office, the India Office, and certain other Departments require approximately 600,000 tons, leaving 1,500,000 tons for con-struction, machinery, and the so-called civilian services of the country, most of which are intimately related to munitions production.

These civilian requirements are mostly for the purpose of the maintenance and repair of plant and works in this country. Among these the upkeep of our railways and rolling-stock is the most important. For some considerable time the supplies to meet these demands have been cut down to the lowest possible figure, and if this is continued for much longer the position is likely to become serious. This, with the 500,000

tons of French steel shipped direct from America, balances a
steel budget of 10,000,000 tons. . . .

7. *Labour.*—The prospective labour requirements resulting
from the preceding Admiralty, War Office, and Aircraft programmes amount in the aggregate to—

Skilled men, 25,000 (10,000 for aircraft).

Unskilled men, 58,000 (40,000 for aircraft and 8,000 for
steel works).

Women, 70,000 (50,000 for aircraft).

In addition to these demands the Admiralty are asking
for 12,500 skilled men and 67,500 unskilled men; the War
Office requires 15,000 artificers, of whom about 8,000 can be
met from among men already in the army, leaving a balance
of 7,000, of whom 5,000–6,000 have still to be supplied by the
Ministry [of Munitions].

To meet the demand for skilled men, the Ministry has at
its disposal a total of 210,000 transferable men, of whom over
50 per cent. are at present employed on important war work.
Even the balance cannot be considered to be immediately
available for transfer, inasmuch as a considerable proportion
of them are engaged in sugar refineries, collieries, food production, and other indispensable occupations.

Nevertheless, the process of dilution is steadily, though
slowly, extending, and as industries are accommodating themselves to the war conditions, the productivity of a given
quantity of labour tends to rise. Since the March Agreement
the Ministry of Munitions have, while continually increasing
output, released 53,000 general service men for the Army as
against 700 released by the Admiralty and 700 from War
Office contracts.

I am therefore advised that, so far as the demand for skilled
labour for the purely munitions programme is concerned, the
requirements can be met without serious dislocation. This is
however subject to the three following conditions:—

(a) A modification of the Admiralty claim that no man
can be transferred from the work on which he is at
present engaged for the Admiralty.

This demand means in effect that the whole of the
skilled labour required for the new shipbuilding pro-

gramme must be drawn exclusively from Munitions
work.

(b) A severe limitation on the demands of the Army for
recruits for artificers corps from among skilled men
working on munitions.

(c) The co-operation of the skilled engineering Unions in a
more extensive dilution on war work. . . .

I do not anticipate any difficulty in finding the women
required.

8. *Explosives.*—This is even more an explosives war than
it is a steel war. Steel is the principal vehicle by which
explosives are conveyed to the enemy. The requirements of
propellant are limited by the production of shell, but there are
other methods, besides those of artillery, of delivering high
explosives to the enemy. The capacity of our existing high-
explosive plant is at present in excess of our shell programme
for 1918. It has been arranged to supplement the present
system of discharging high explosives by providing up to a
maximum 1,000 tons a week of bombs to be dropped from
aeroplanes. The possibility of extending the Trench Mortar
offensive power of our Army is also being examined. To utilise
fully our existing high-explosive plants it is necessary that we
should ship from Chile approximately 788,000 tons of nitrates;
at present the tonnage for only 600,000 has provisionally been
agreed upon.

New and very serious demands for T.N.T. are also being
made by the Admiralty for mines.

9. *Chemical Warfare.*—G.H.Q. has asked that we should
add an irritant gas to our lethal and lachrymatory gases.
Development of this new branch of chemical warfare will
take many months and cannot come fully into play until the
end of next year's campaign. Using all possible resources of
chemical shell with existing types of chemical, we could supply
the army next year with 2½ times the quantity of gas shell
supplied in the 1917 campaign.

If the present scheme for the new gas matures, the whole
supply of chemical shell would be four times as great by the
end of 1918 as in 1917.

10. *Guns and Ammunition.*—On the above basis of steel
and explosives, together with importations of finished shells
and components, it will be impossible to meet the Commander-

in-Chief's full demand both for guns and shells as set out in his letter of the 17th July. . . .

11. Before rejoicing at these facts it is necessary to compare the British, French, and German artilleries. During 1917 the French and ourselves have maintained about an equal number of combatants in the line in France, and we have done the harder fighting. The French had however on the 1st October 10,000 guns to our 6,000 guns, ours, on the whole, being heavier and newer. The new French heavy artillery programme is now coming into bearing, and from now on they anticipate very large monthly deliveries. By April 1918 the French will have 9,000 guns, all modern and steadily increasing. Our comparable figure in the field in France will be approaching 8,000, which is the maximum establishment that our army has at present arranged for. Our infantry will not therefore be quite so well supported with artillery as the French.

The War Office state that the Germans had in 1917—

	Guns.
On the French front	12,432
On the Russian front	5,176
Balkans and Italy	808
Total	18,416 [1]

The balance on the Western front was as follows:—

Franco-British	15,969
German	12,432

But though we had a superiority in numbers, the Germans had superior weight of metal. Deducting from each side field guns, in which we are greatly superior, the balance in heavier and more important weapons stood as follows:—

Franco-British	6,654
German	7,568

[1] General von Wrisberg, Head of the Principal Department of the Prussian War Ministry, in his book *Heer und Heimath* (Army and Home) published in 1924, p. 58, says: 'The greatest number of [German] heavy guns on the front was in February 1917: Heavy, 7,130. Field guns and Field howitzers, 10,836. Total 17,966.'

This is a remarkable instance of the accuracy of the British War Office information.

If the new British and French programmes are carried out punctually we should have in the West by April, 1918 17,000 modern and 2,000 older guns with steady increases in prospect.

The Germans will have their present 12,432 guns, plus—

(a) Any new programme they are making.
(b) Any of the 5,176 guns they may choose to take from the Russian front.
(c) Any of the 2,000 or 3,000 guns recently captured from the Russians or Italians.

It is certain therefore that with our utmost efforts, and under the most favourable conditions, we cannot expect any superiority in guns next year.

It does not follow however that the ammunition for all the German guns will be as abundant as ours.

Nor on the other hand, being on the defensive, need they use it so copiously or continuously.

All these facts appear to me to be worthy of profound consideration.

12. The most striking deficiency in the British artillery is found in very heavy long-range guns. On the 1st October the position was as follows:—

Very heavy guns (9.2-in. and 12-in.)—

German								180
French								175
British								6

There is only one source to which we can look to improve the long-range battery at the disposal of our troops, viz., the Navy.

If we could receive from Naval sources and from our Fortresses during the next six months 100 heavy guns (including 30 already promised), i.e., 14-inch, new 13.5 inch, or 12-inch of all marks, and 100 medium guns, i.e., 10-inch and 9.2-inch, it would be possible, without prejudice to the programmes, to make a very substantial addition to the British long-range heavy artillery.

I ask that this may be earnestly examined.

13. *Aeroplanes.*—It is understood that the programme of the Royal Flying Corps provides for the equipment of the following:—

By December 1917, 85 active squadrons.
By March   1918, 106   "   "
By June   1918, 149   "   "
By December   1918, 200   "   "

This programme, together with a total of 3,000 aeroplanes required by the R.N.A.S. by August 1918 and 9,500 by the R.F.C. for training purposes, involves a total production by that date of between 27,000 and 28,000 machines of all kinds. In order to obtain this result our output in the summer of 1918 should be at the rate of 2,700 per month. . . .

14. *Tanks.*—Tanks have never yet been used in numbers under conditions favourable to their action. Nor have we ever yet had a sufficiently reliable kind of tank, nor nearly enough of them. If they have held their own in 1917 it has been under adverse circumstances, both in their production here and their use in France.

In consequence the Army consider that they cannot allocate more than 18,500 men to the tank corps. This limits the number of fighting tanks required to an establishment of 1,080 with ample maintenance and a certain number of supply and gun-carrying tanks.

There will be no difficulty in supplying this requirement, but the new designs will not be available in full numbers until July, 1918. Thereafter considerable expansions would be possible. The demand made by tanks on steel and skilled labour is small and does not sensibly affect either shipbuilding or aeroplanes.

15. *Dollars.*—We have been forced by the shortage of Canadian and American dollars to reduce our orders in Canada and the United States, to considerably lower figures than hitherto. Shell-producing and explosives plants have had to be demobilised in Canada almost as soon as they had been called into being, and thus we have had to do without most valuable additions to our resources for which labour and material were available. We cannot buy more than 8 millions sterling a month on the average in 1918 from the United States, instead of an average of 13 millions in the first half of 1917; nor more than 6 millions a month in Canada, compared to 9½ millions. This curtailment of our resources must be borne in mind.

16. To sum up, the present adverse factors to munitions production are as follows:—

(i) The increasing demands of the Admiralty.
(ii) The general shortage of labour (especially skilled labour) and the risk of pressing labour hard at the present time.
(iii) The curtailment of our orders in Canada and the United States on financial grounds.
(iv) The low level to which we have been compelled to restrict our iron ore importations.

On the other hand, the immense new plants begun in the first year of the Ministry of Munitions are being utilised to their full advantage and are steadily developing their output of various munitions.

The power of massed production and the increasing efficiency of diluted and female labour, together with the accumulation of working stocks and adequate reserves and the progressive elimination of commercial work, render possible a large increase in the total output so long as the necessary tonnage and labour required are forthcoming.

17. In spite therefore of the difficulties, it should still be possible, by taking the proper measures of organisation, by enforcing the necessary economies, and by utilizing to the full the resources of every department without exception, to meet and satisfy the main demands that are made upon us.

There still remain as new objectives of effort within the bounds of possibility and without undue prejudice to the above:—

(i) Increased long-range aeroplane bombing power.
(ii) Increased long-range mobile and semi-mobile heavy artillery.
(iii) Increased trench-mortar offensive.
(iv) Increased tank development late in the year.
(v) Increased chemical warfare supplies.

18. There are however four principles which must be accepted and resolutely applied:—

(i) The tonnage utilized for non-military imports of all kinds, including to some extent food, must be cut down.

(ii) The Admiralty must endeavour to find the bulk of its own skilled labour for shipbuilding from its own extensive resources, and it must subject every part of its immense organisation to a loyal and searching scrutiny in the general interest.

(iii) The dormant man-power of the units of the Home army must be made effective as an aid to transport, industry, and agriculture.

(iv) The business of supply must be properly co-ordinated. We cannot afford the waste which arises from the independent and competitive action of individual departments.

No sooner had we completed the Munitions Budget, with its innumerable apportionments and orders, than the startling news arrived that the Inter-Allied Commission on Food Supplies, on which the War Cabinet was represented, had allocated, at the earnest request of the French Minister of Commerce, no less than two million tons of freight for the transport of additional food for France and Italy. Nearly the whole—1,550,000 tons—had to be cut off the Munitions share. I reacted violently against this. The threat to France and Italy of drastic reductions in the steel we had promised them enlisted the active aid of the Munitions Ministers of both countries. A considerable portion of these self-indulgent importations were eventually cancelled. But heavy cuts had to be made in shell steel, and the Army was warned to expect a reduced programme.

The outlook and the immediate pressure led me, in my own sphere, to seek by every shift and from every quarter to increase our steel resources on which the British armies depended. No doubt from the higher position of the War Cabinet a more general view of relative requirements could be taken, and my appeals and protests imply no criticism of others. It was my duty above all to keep Sir Douglas Haig supplied with every requisite, and at this we slaved and struggled from daybreak to midnight. We were well ahead

with shells of nearly every kind. We were well ahead with
rifles and rifle ammunition. During all the autumn the armies
had had all the shell they demanded, but the prolonged firing
of Paschendale and the destruction of battle had so seriously
worn out our field and medium artillery that guns had become
the limiting factor. Immense replacements and repairs had
to be made in the brief interval between November and the
spring.

To the Chancellor of the Exchequer.

November 25, 1917.

The position which has been created by the surrender of
2,000,000 tons of shipping to the food supply of France and
the consequent reduction on Munitions imports (almost
exclusively steel and iron ore) of upwards of 1,550,000 tons,
is so disastrous in its consequences upon the offensive power of
the British armies next year, and indeed upon our whole war-
making capacity, that I cannot accept it without using every
conceivable effort to minimise the disaster. If the *volume*
of our tonnage is to be reduced, it is indispensable that the
value of it should, as far as possible, be enhanced. This
raises the whole Canadian position. There is no more melancholy chapter in the history of British Munitions Supply than
the laborious creation of large and vitally needed shell plants
in Canada, only for them to be dispersed and destroyed at
the moment they have come into bearing. . . . Shortage
of dollars, and dollars only, was the cause of this misfortune. . . .
Surely the truth ought to be known, and further efforts made
to avert the loss which is impending. There could be no more
short-sighted and even mad policy than to damp down and
break up these Canadian plants at the very time when the increasing demands of the United States for their own armies
threaten to exclude us very largely from that field. I am now
confronted both with American proposals for placing orders in
Canadian Munition Factories, and with additional offers of
shell and other essential munitions from Canada. Are you
really going to be content to let this all go by the board?
Here for instance are proposals from the Governor-General
of Canada to utilise the Ross Rifle Factory for the manufacture of machine-gun barrels. This would be of the greatest

service to us. Both the Colonial Office and the Governor-General are pressing for a reply. Again, there is an offer for 25,000 6-inch shells a week additional from Canada. These are the shells which are most needed by our troops at the present time, in regard to which I have just received a fresh demand for 2,000,000 from the Commander-in-Chief. The machinery in Canada is available, the labour is available, the material is available—the need is most grave. Are we really to let the plant be scattered and the machines to drift over piecemeal into the United States and so cut ourselves off for-ever from this source of highly portable munitions of the most necessary character? I know how great your difficulties are and how strenuous have been the exertions which you have made to procure us larger credits, but I really cannot accept this decision departmentally from the Treasury and make myself the agent of its announcement. It seems to me that the responsibility in a matter of this kind could only be assumed by the War Cabinet, and I hope you will not mind my asking that the matter should definitely be brought before them. Neither in man-power nor in war material are we put-ting out our full energies, and having regard to the reserves which the Germans will be able to bring back in both troops and artillery next year from the Russian front, the position of our armies may be most serious. Perhaps in the first instance we could have a small private conference at the Treasury, to which I would bring various experts.

To Sir Joseph Maclay (Controller of Shipping).

November 25, 1917.

You must pardon my anxiety about the importations of iron ore. The decisions which have been taken without my being even informed, to give 2,000,000 tons of shipping to the French and Italian food supply, have shattered our means of furnishing the armies in the field with the am-munition they require for 1918. They will also force me to notify to the French and Italians an entire suspension of the allocation to them of steel products of all kinds, although used exclusively for military purposes. This will unques-tionably create a serious diplomatic position. I was informed in Paris that the French were astonished at the liberality of our concessions to them in the matter of food.

It is scarcely possible to do justice to the disastrous position created by the cut of 1,550,000 tons on munition imports, and the lamentable crippling of our otherwise available resources in war power which that entails. Can you wonder therefore that I am exerting myself by every means to procure some amelioration of this state of things? I am advised by experts of unimpeachable authority that ferro-concrete barges of a seaworthy character could have been constructed many months ago and that they could have been so employed as to afford a direct relief to certain classes of tonnage. Even now I do not think they are being sufficiently developed. Only 70 I understand have been ordered, whereas at least double the number are required. A deficiency of British shipping and our liberality to our Allies may not be our business at the Ministry of Munitions, but it is undoubtedly our misfortune. As it is, the plans of the Commander-in-Chief are being vitiated and the offensive power of the British armies very seriously impaired. I say nothing of the economic difficulties which will be created in England through the failure to maintain the Railways and other essential Civil Services through the deficiency of steel.

To Monsieur Loucheur (Minister of Armaments, France).

November 25, 1917.

I have referred your letter of the 20th of November to the study of the departments concerned, and I will communicate with you as soon as I have their observations on its detail. The whole steel situation in Great Britain has however been revolutionised by the decision to allocate 2,000,000 tons of British shipping to carry food supplies to France and Italy. The direct consequence of this has been to reduce the estimated importation for the Ministry of Munitions by 1,550,000 tons up to the present time, and practically the whole of this is taken from our importations of ore and of steel. It is therefore quite impossible for me to continue to supply the 40,000 tons of various steel products to France as previously agreed between us. I have to impose the most severe reductions on the supply of ammunition for the British armies, reducing the weight of shell to be fired in 1918 by between half a million and 750,000 tons, and a further very severe reduction has to be imposed upon our already depleted railway and other vital domestic services. In these circumstances, I can only supply France with steel products in 1918 to the extent to which tonnage is placed at my disposal in abatement of the 1,550,000 tons reduction. If, for instance, it is in your power to procure a retrocession of half a million or 300,000 tons of tonnage allocated to French food stuffs, I can continue my supplies of steel to that extent, as the liberated tonnage will be used to bring in the necessary quantities of ore and steel to us. But failing this or some similar arrangement, it is absolutely impossible for me, with the tonnage allocated at present, to continue supplies of steel for French purposes. I am of course making a similar communication to the Italian Government so far as next year is concerned, and apart from the immediate measures which are required to meet the emergency caused by their disaster.

I should add that if the position improves from any cause, and especially from a reduction in the net weekly loss by submarine sinkings, I shall of course be ready to contribute towards your programmes to the best of my ability.

While awaiting the results of this outcry, it was necessary to face the facts. I gave the following instructions:—

Secretary.
S.
M.
Clamping Committee.[1]

November 25, 1917.

The cut in the importations of iron ore is so serious that every effort must be made to mitigate its consequences. There must be great masses of iron in one form and another scattered about the country. Take for instance all the park and area railings. I should suppose there were 20,000 tons of iron in the Hyde Park railings alone, while the weight of metal in the area railings of the London streets must be enormous. The same is true of many great towns throughout the country. Then there is the building material of unfinished buildings, girders, etc. which could be worked up into other urgently needed Works of Construction for military purposes. A few strands of barbed wire could be used to

[1] So called by me because it was charged with fitting the programme together.

protect areas and enclosed parks. Drastic action will help to rouse people to a sense of the emergency and of the magnitude of the effort required. Thirdly, there are the battlefields. There must be 700,000 or 800,000 tons of shell-steel lying about on the Somme battlefields alone. The collection of this is vital. The proper machines must be constructed. A smelting plant should be set up on the battlefields.

Let me have definite recommendations for immediate action on all these points with the least possible delay, and advise me as to the composition of a suitable committee, not consisting of members of Council, which can carry out any policy decided on.

Clamping Committee.
November 26, 1917.

You should recast the Programme on the following assumptions:—

(1) That the armies in France only fire in 1918 the same weight of shell as they fired in 1917.

(2) That all additional shell that our iron and steel import permits of should be stored for a 1919 climax.

(3) That explosives needs will be reduced by the reduction on the Programme of artillery firing.

(4) That the Trench Mortar offensive will be limited to 25,000 tons additional.

(5) That the Army do not want the semi-mobile mountings and that about 30 firing points on railway mountings will be sufficient to wear out all the guns we are likely to get from the Navy.

(6) That the manufacture of Tanks of various designs must be pushed to the extreme limit.

(7) That an additional programme of aeroplanes will be necessary.

(8) That the process of substitution and dilution must be continued to release at least 100,000 A-1 men.

(9) That the manufacture of guns should be carried on at full blast during the whole of 1918.

(10) That the shell plant which will have been somewhat damped down in 1918 should be opened out to the full in 1919.

(11) That our Munitions Programme should be harmonised with those of France, Italy, and the United States, so as to secure the maximum production.

(12) That we cannot count on more than a minimum of 11,000,000 tons delivered here during the 12 months, and must not promise to other Departments anything based on a larger delivery. Probably we shall get more. in which case it will be easy to do better than our word.

To the War Cabinet.

December 31, 1917.

I must draw the attention of the Cabinet to the serious character of the problems of steel supply now presented for their decision.

The revised Munitions Budget which has been circulated involves a heavy reduction upon the Ammunition Programme on which the Commander-in-Chief and the War Office have been counting, not less than 500,000 tons which we could have made into shells having been deducted from it. I had urged as a measure of precaution that we should be permitted to place orders in the United States for 1,000,000 tons of steel, of which 500,000 is needed this year for the reduced programme, and the other 500,000 would afford a reserve on which we could draw sooner or later according to tonnage conditions. We are now told that we cannot place these orders. If this decision is to stand, the Shell Programme of the armies must undergo further serious reduction. We are cut off from Spanish ore by [want of] tonnage and from American steel by [want of] dollars. In both cases food imports for ourselves or for our Allies are displacing ton for ton metal which could otherwise be fired at the enemy—for which, that is to say, shell factories, the fuses, the filling plants, the guns and the gunners are all available.

At the same time we have been forced to break up Canadian shell plants as soon as they have been laboriously called into being and had begun deliveries, on account of the failure of the Canadian Government or of the Treasury or of both to make the necessary financial arrangements. On top of this we are now confronted with the proposal to cut our Canadian allocation of dollars from 30,000,000 to 20,000,000 per month. . . .

Thirdly, the Admiralty demand for steel in all its forms is already enormous and continues to increase.

In these circumstances it is surely our duty to make vigorous and genuine efforts to sustain the artillery of the British Army with the necessary supplies of ammunition, and not to acquiesce in its being cut down whenever a difficulty of tonnage or dollars or food supply is involved.

To the War Cabinet.

November 11, 1917.

We ought to endeavour to gain and keep the control of the war to which our strength entitles us, using that strength to sustain our Allies without allowing them to lose their self-reliance. We should be careful not to dissipate our strength or melt it down to the average level of exhausted nations. It will be better used with design by us than weakly dispersed. *Resolute to expend everything for the common cause, we ought not to shrink from being taskmasters.* I deprecate most strongly our making any general agreement in regard to Munitions and raw materials similar to that which has been made about food. On the contrary, I would continue to make *ad hoc* allocations when particular emergencies are shown, always exacting where possible some other services or accommodation in return. There must at any rate be one strong power to face Germany in 1918. To strike an average in these matters, to bind oneself in advance to some system of 'share and share alike,' and thus to deprive ourselves of all our power of giving when need arises, may be logic—it may even be equity—but it is not the way to win the war.

In the end all finished happily. The Shipping Controller proved better than his word. The U-boat pressure weakened and several million tons more freight became in fact available than his caution had allowed. We too were found to have somewhat larger resources than we had thought it right to parade. As will be seen as the account proceeds, the Ministry of Munitions were found capable not only of fulfilling their original programmes, but of meeting a gigantic emergency for which no formal provision had been made. 'As regards material,' wrote Sir Douglas Haig in his final despatch in 1919, 'it was not until midsummer, 1916, that the artillery situation became even approximately adequate to the conduct

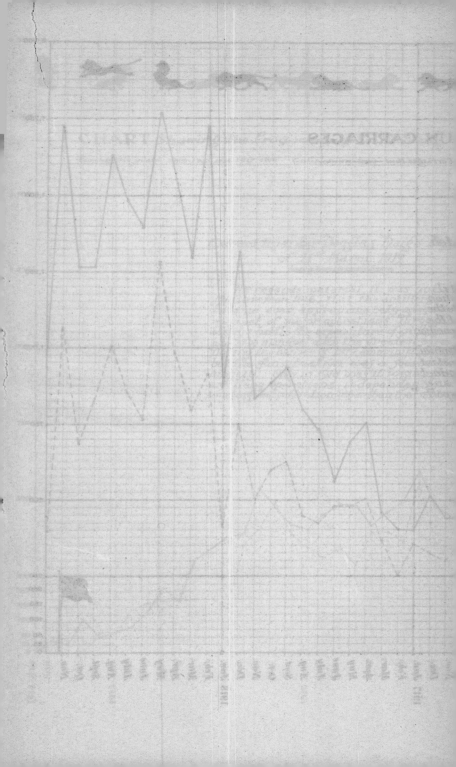

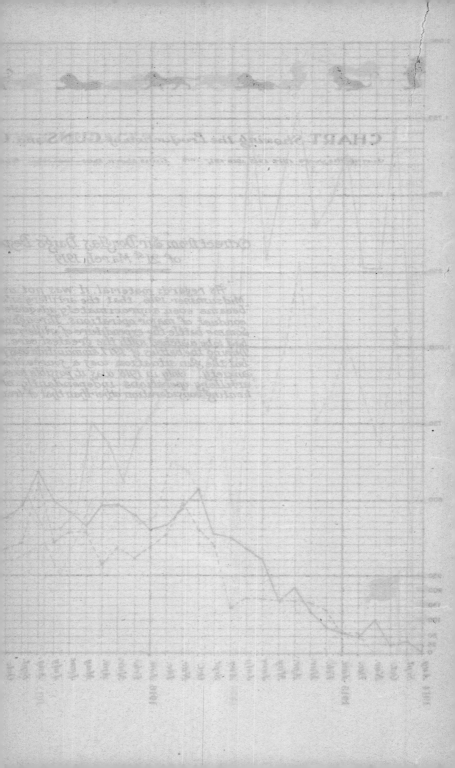

of major operations. Throughout the Somme battle the expenditure of artillery ammunition had to be watched with the greatest care. During the battles of 1917 ammunition was plentiful, but the gun situation was a source of constant anxiety. Only in 1918 was it possible to conduct artillery operations independently of any limiting consideration other than that of transport.'

CHAPTER XIV

THE AUTUMN STRUGGLE

AT the time I rejoined the Government the British armies were on the eve of a new tremendous offensive. The long-prepared attack upon the Messines ridge had been executed with precision and success on June 7, and Sir Douglas Haig's further plan was to strike from the direction of Ypres towards Ostend. This was in fact a revival on a gigantic scale and by different methods of those ideas of clearing the sea flank by which Sir John French had been so much attracted in 1914. Forty divisions had been assembled between Kemmel Hill and the Belgian front. Mountains of ammunition had been accumulated, and the strongest concentration of artillery ever yet developed was to sustain the attack. The British Headquarters were as usual confident of a decisive success, and as usual they were stoutly supported by Sir William Robertson and the General Staff at the War Office. On the other hand, the positions to be assaulted were immensely strong. The enemy was fully prepared. The frowning undulations of the Paschendale-Klercken ridge had been fortified with every resource of German science and ingenuity. The ground was studded with ferro-concrete block-houses, 'Pill Boxes' as they were soon called, crammed with machine guns, lapped in barbed wire, and impenetrable to the heaviest bombardment. The railway communications behind the enemy's front were at least as good as, if not indeed superior to, those which maintained the British offensive. A German army containing three times as many divisions as were required at any given moment to hold the ground had been assembled under Prince Rupprecht, and every facility for the relief and replacement of exhausted units had been carefully studied. The Dutch railways carried ceaseless supplies of gravel for the concrete, and the elaboration of the defences line behind line proceeded continually.

Apart from the hopes of decisive victory, which grew with every step away from the British front line and reached absolute conviction in the Intelligence Department, two reasons were adduced by General Headquarters to justify the renewed severe demand upon the troops. First the alleged exhausted and quiescent condition of the French Army since the defeat of General Nivelle's April offensive; secondly the importance of taking Ostend and Zeebrugge in order to paralyse or cripple the U-boat war. The first of these arguments was exaggerated. The French Army was no doubt saving its strength as much as possible, but the casualty tables show that during 1917 they inflicted nearly as many losses on the Germans as did our own troops. The U-boat argument was wholly fallacious. A grave responsibility rests upon the Admiralty for misleading Haig and his Staff about the value of Ostend and Zeebrugge to the submarine campaign. These two ports were convenient advanced bases for U-boats working in the English Channel, but they were in no way indispensable to the submarine war. Submarines able to go completely around the British Isles and to remain at sea a whole month at a time could work almost as easily from their own home bases in the Elbe, the Weser, and the Ems, as from the advanced and much-battered harbours of Belgium. The whole U-boat war was based on the main German naval harbours, and was never dependent on anything else. In fact in May, 1918, the month after both Ostend and Zeebrugge had been sealed up by the Navy, the U-boat sinkings actually showed an increase over the preceding month in which they were open and in full activity. Whatever influence this erroneous argument may have had upon the Haig-Robertson decision to launch a new offensive, it certainly contributed to baffle the objections of the Prime Minister and the War Cabinet. It seemed to throw the army into the struggle against the submarines. It confused the issue, it darkened counsel, it numbed misgivings, overpowered the dictates of prudence, and cleared the way for a forlorn expenditure of valour and life without equal in futility.

In the war against Turkey in the south-eastern theatre the most costly and laborious policy was also pursued. The Turks, fortified between the desert and the sea at Gaza under Jemal Pasha, confronted successfully the British Army under Allenby, which had toiled forward by railway and water-pipe line from Egypt at extreme exertion and expense. This obstacle was surmounted or destroyed in the following year. Meanwhile however the obvious manœuvre of landing an army behind the Turks was dismissed by Sir William Robertson as venturesome and impracticable.

Even before I joined his Government the Prime Minister, as I have written, used to discuss the war situation with me freely. On my taking office he made me acquainted with everything. After his excursion with General Nivelle and its disillusionments, he had returned to those views against seeking offensives on the Western Front without the necessary superiority or method, with which the reader is familiar. The peak of the U-boat sinkings seemed to have been surmounted. If on land hopes had been dupes, fears at sea had also been liars. Mr. Lloyd George was now content to await in the main theatre the arrival of the American armies. He wished Sir Douglas Haig to maintain an active defensive for the rest of the year and to nurse his strength. Meanwhile activity in Palestine and the reinforcement of Italy by British and French divisions might produce important results against Turkey and Austria, and would in any case not be unduly costly in life. At first the majority of the War Cabinet shared these general opinions. But between right thought and right action there was a gulf. Sir William Robertson, and under his direction the General Staff at the War Office, pressed unceasingly for further immediate exertions. Their insistence gained several adherents in the Cabinet. All through June the discussions were maintained. In the end the Prime Minister did not feel strong enough to face the Haig-Robertson combination. He submitted with resentful fatalism. The plan of sustaining Italy was dropped, and by the third week of July Robertson had extorted from the Cabinet and conveyed to Haig an assurance of 'whole-hearted' support[1] for the Paschendale attack. When I had the opportunity of learning the facts it was too late. The decision had already been taken. My only hope was to limit the consequences. On July 22 I gave my counsel as follows:—

Mr. Churchill to the Prime Minister.

Many thanks for letting me see these most interesting papers which I return herewith. Broadly speaking I agree with Smuts. But I deplore with you the necessity for giving way to the military wish for a renewed offensive in the West. The armies are equal. If anything, the Germans are the stronger. They have larger reserves and ample munitions. An endless series of fortified lines with all kinds of flooding possibilities and great natural difficulties of ground constitute insuperable obstacles. We already approach the end of July. Even if three or four battles as good as Messines are won, the situation in the West will not be appreciably altered by the end of the year.

It is clear however that no human power exists which can stop the attempt being made. The essential thing now is to

[1] Robertson, *Soldiers and Statesmen*, Vol. II, p. 249.

arrive at a definition of success and 'great results' which will enable a new decision to be taken after the first or second phases of this offensive have been fought. Such a definition must, it seems to me, involve three conditions, viz. objectives taken; casualties sustained; and thirdly (very important) the time taken or required between any one thrust and the next. Thus it should be possible, by reference to these forecasts, to settle definitely after (say) six weeks of fighting whether there really is any prospect of obtaining 'great results' before winter sets in. Unless you can arrive at something definite on these points, your Italian project, with which I cordially agree, will simply be put off from day to day until it is too late. Remember how Joffre behaved about the four divisions which were to go to the Asiatic shore of the Dardanelles as soon as he knew whether he was going to achieve decisive results in the Champagne battle in 1915.

It is worth also remembering that the best of all feints, and the most deceptive, is a real attack which you subsequently decide not to carry through; the reserves for which are suddenly thrown into quite a different theatre.

With regard to the East, the truth is staring us in the face. An army of six divisions, British or Franco-British, should be taken from [the] Salonica [front] and put in behind Jemal's army. This will force that army to surrender, and all the allied troops in Syria and Palestine, including Allenby's, would be free by the spring of next year for action in Italy or France. The mere concentration of five or six divisions in Salonica, as they were gradually replaced on the front by fresh [Greek] arrivals, would impart to the Salonica army a speculative value it has wholly lost. It would be crouched instead of sprawled. They could stay in Salonica training and recuperating until the season of a potential Russo-Roumanian offensive had passed, collecting aquatic transport meanwhile. All the time they would be threatening the enemy in a dozen places. It will be a thousand pities if this or something like it cannot be done.

Don't get torpedoed; for if I am left alone your colleagues will eat me.

The Prime Minister went so far as to offer the command of the British armies in Palestine to General Smuts. After deliberation Smuts replied that he was willing to accept the task on one condition, namely that he should be allowed to land an adequate army to cut the Turkish communications. As this project was not considered open, he declined the command. But in his place was found a leader whose personality and skill were equal to the task of dislodging and ultimately of destroying the Turkish armies in Syria without the aid of a great amphibious operation. With the appointment of Allenby the whole situation in Palestine was rapidly transformed. Although he repeatedly demanded more reinforcements than could be spared, and prudently dwelt on the difficulties before him, Allenby by a series of masterly combinations succeeded with smaller forces both in out-manœuvring and in out-fighting the Turks under Jemal, advised by Falkenhayn. Feinting at Gaza in the last week of October, he stormed Beersheba by a surprise attack of two infantry divisions and a wide turning movement of cavalry and camelry. Having thus gained the enemy's desert flank, he rolled up from the eastward in a succession of fierce actions the strongly fortified Turkish lines. Gaza was taken on November 6: 10,000 Turks had been made prisoners, and at least as many killed and wounded: and a vigorous pursuit opened the port of Jaffa to the further supply of the British forces. Thus possessed of the coastal region, a new base, and an alternative short line of communication, Allenby advanced north-westward upon Jerusalem, continuing to drive the Seventh and Eighth Turkish Armies before him and compromising the eventual retreat of the Fourth. On December 8, 1917, the Turks abandoned Jerusalem after 400 years of blighting occupation, and the British Commander-in-Chief entered the city amid the acclamations of the inhabitants. Here he maintained himself in a situation of much delicacy throughout the winter, re-grouping his forces, wisely fostering the Arab revolt which grew around the astonishing personality of Lawrence, and preparing for even larger enterprises in the spring. With no more than 150,000 men he

had expelled 170,000 German-led Turkish troops from fortified positions—Plevnas—on which years of labour had been
spent, and had inflcted upon them most serious losses in
men, guns and territory.

No praise is too high for these brilliant and frugal operations,
which will long serve as a model in theatres of war in which
manœuvre is possible. Nevertheless their results did not
simplify the general problem. On the contrary, by opening
up a competing interest which could not influence the main
decision, they even complicated it. The very serious drain of
men, munitions and transport which flowed unceasingly to the
Palestine Expedition ought to have been arrested by action
far swifter in character and far larger in scale. Brevity and
finality, not less at this period than throughout the war, were
the true tests of any diversion against Turkey. Prolonged and
expanding operations in distant unrelated theatres, whether
they languished as at Salonica, or crackled briskly and
brightly forward under Allenby in Palestine, were not to be
reconciled with a wise war policy. It would have been far
safer and far cheaper in life and resources to run a greater
risk for a shorter time. The advantage of the command of the
sea should not have been neglected. If, while Allenby held
the Turks at Gaza, a long-prepared descent had been made at
Haifa or elsewhere on the sea coast behind them, and if the
railway by which alone they could exist had been severed in
September by a new army of six or eight divisions, the war in
Syria would have been ended at a stroke. The Eastern drain
on our resources would have been stopped from February
onwards; all the British troops in Palestine would have been
available to meet the supreme peril in France. But in Palestine
as formerly at Gallipoli, the clash of the Western and Eastern
schools of thought produced incoherence and half-measures.
Enough was sent East to be a dangerous dispersion, and never
at one time enough to compel a prompt conclusion. It will be
incredible to future generations that the strategists of an island

people then blessed with the unique and sovereign attribute of Sea Power should, throughout the whole of the Great War, have failed so utterly to turn it to offensive profit.

In the actual event, as will be seen, Ludendorff's offensive of 1918 dissipated in a day all Allenby's careful plans for the spring campaign. Not less than sixty battalions with many batteries were incontinently snatched from Palestine to plug the shot hole of the twenty-first of March; and his depleted army remained till two Indian divisions arrived from Mesopotamia in August, in an extremely precarious position. That from such circumstances, he should have contrived the captures of Deraa, Damascus and Aleppo, and the destruction of every vestige of Turkish power in Syria, military and civil before the armistice, is one of the most remarkable achievements of the war.

*   *   *   *   *

Meanwhile the British offensive against Paschendale unrolled its sombre fate. The terrific artillery pulverized the ground, smashing simultaneously the German trenches and the ordinary drainage. By sublime devotion and frightful losses small indentations were made upon the German front. In six weeks at the farthest point we had advanced four miles. Soon the rain descended, and the vast crater fields became a sea of choking fetid mud in which men, animals and tanks floundered and perished hopelessly. The few tracks which alone could be preserved across this morass were swept with ceaseless shell fire, through which endless columns of transport marched with fortitude all night long. The impossibility of supplying the British field and medium batteries with ammunition at any distance from the only road maintained in being, led to their being massed in line by its side. Thus there could be no concealment, and the German counter-fire caused very heavy losses in gunners and guns and killed nearly all the artillery horses.

The disappointing captures of ground were relieved by tales of prodigious German slaughter. The losses and anxieties inflicted upon the enemy must not be underrated. Ludendorff's admissions are upon record. These violent sustained thrusts shook the enemy to their foundations. But the German losses were always on a far smaller scale. They always had far fewer troops in the cauldron. They always took nearly two lives for one and sold every inch of ground with extortion.

Further efforts were made during October by the Prime Minister to bring the operations to an end. He went so far as to call Sir Henry Wilson and Lord French into counsel as 'technical advisers' of the Cabinet, independent of the General Staff. We have the tale naïvely published by Robertson himself.[1] Lord French, we are told, after criticising 'in twenty pages out of twenty-six' the Haig-Robertson strategy and tactics, recommended that we should 'stand everywhere on the defensive, only resorting to such offensive action as would make the defensive effective; await the development of the forces of the United States; and in the meantime rely upon a drastic economic war to weaken the enemy.' In formally consulting outside advisers the Prime Minister obviously courted the resignation of the Chief of the Imperial General Staff. It was not forthcoming. The Cabinet were not prepared to demand it; and nothing but mutual mistrust resulted.

Accordingly in Flanders the struggle went on. New divisions continued to replace those that were shattered. The rain descended and the mud sea spread. Still the will power of the Commander and the discipline of the Army remained invincible. By measureless sacrifices Paschendale was won. But beyond, far beyond, still rose intact and unapproachable the fortifications of Klercken. August had passed away; September was gone; October was far spent. The full

[1] Robertson, *Soldiers and Statesmen*, Vol. II, pp. 256 *et seq.*

severity of a Flanders winter gripped the ghastly battlefield. Ceaselessly the Menin gate of Ypres disgorged its streams of manhood. Fast as the cannons fired, the ammunition behind them flowed in faster. Even in October the British Staff were planning and launching offensives and were confident of reaching the goal of decisive results. It was not until the end of November that final failure was accepted. '*Boche* is bad and *Boue* is bad,' said Foch, then little more than an observer of events, 'but *Boche* and *Boue* together . . . Ah!' He held up warning hands.

It cannot be said that 'the soldiers,' that is to say the Staff, did not have their way. They tried their sombre experiment to its conclusion. They took all they required from Britain. They wore down alike the manhood and the guns of the British Army almost to destruction. They did it in the face of the plainest warnings, and of arguments which they could not answer. Sir Douglas Haig acted from conviction; but Sir William Robertson drifted ponderously. He has accepted the main responsibility. He could not well avoid it. 'I was more than a mere adviser. I was the professional head of all the British Armies, as Haig was of those in France. They looked to me, as did the whole Empire, to see that they were not asked to do impossible things, and were not in any way placed at a disadvantage unnecessarily.'[1] And again (June 23), 'My own responsibility . . . is not small in urging the continuance of a plan regarding which he [the Prime Minister] has grave misgivings . . .'[2] And lastly (Robertson to Haig, Sept. 27), 'My own views are known to you. They have always been "defensive" in all theatres but the West. But the difficulty is to *prove* the wisdom of this now that Russia is out. I confess I stick to it more because I see nothing better, and because my instinct prompts me to stick to it, than because of any good argument by which I can support

[1] Robertson, *Soldiers and Statesmen*, Vol. I, p. 188.
[2] *Ibid.*, Vol. II, p. 247.

it.'[1] These are terrible words when used to sustain the sacrifices of nearly four hundred thousand men.

Meanwhile the results of neglecting Italy for the sake of Paschendale exploded with a violence which no one could have foreseen. On October 24 began the Italian disaster of Caporetto. Six German divisions were brought swiftly to the Isonzo by night marches and concealed in deep valleys behind the front. These and the presence of General von Below animated the large Austrian armies. A skilful attack by mountain roads gained a key position. A sudden bombardment by heavy artillery and gas shells, followed by a general assault along the whole front led at the decisive points by German troops, aided by the effects of defeatist propaganda within the Italian lines, produced in twelve hours a complete and decisive defeat of General Cadorna's army. By nightfall more than a million Italians were in full retreat. A large portion of the army passed into dissolution. In three days 200,000 men and 1,800 guns were captured, and before the long retreat was finished and the Italian front had been reconstituted 80 miles to the westward along the Piave, upwards of 800,000 soldiers through death, wounds, sickness, capture, desertion, and above all disappearance, had been torn from the Italian standards. This astounding disaster required immediate exertions by Britain and France.

I was resting at my house in Kent when authentic news arrived. The Prime Minister telephoned to me to motor at once to Walton Heath. He showed me the telegrams, which even in their guarded form revealed a defeat of the first magnitude. At this moment when our army had been bled white at Paschendale and when the French were still recovering from the Nivelle offensive and its disquieting consequences, the prospect of having to make a large detachment of force for Italy was uninviting. The Prime Minister reacted with his accustomed resiliency. He set off in a few days to Rapallo, where he had proposed a meeting with the French and Italian

[1] Robertson, *Soldiers and Statesmen*, Vol. II, p. 255.

political and military chiefs. Meanwhile five French and five British divisions under General Fayolle and Sir Herbert Plumer, two of the most successful and experienced Commanders on the Western Front, were moved with the utmost rapidity through the tunnels under the Alps, and began to appear from the 10th of November onwards upon the Italian front. Had they been sent a few months earlier, it is certain, even if the Ally Italian offensive had not yielded important results, that events would have followed an entirely different course.

The greatness of the Italian nation shone forth in an hour which recalled the morrow of Cannae. 'Defeatism' withered in the flame of national resolve. Immense as had been the Italian losses, the war effort of Italy was far greater from Caporetto onwards than in the earlier period of the war. Ruthless punishment restored the discipline of the armies: ardent reserves and volunteers refilled their ranks. But all this took time, and for several months the fate of Italy hung in the balance. It was necessary to contemplate a situation in which the North of Italy might be completely overrun by Teutonic armies; when Italy might be beaten out of the war, and when the development of a Swiss front might have been imposed upon France. Mercifully 'the trees do not grow up to the sky,' and offensives however successful lose their pristine force satiated with the ground they gain.

What would have happened had Germany prepared from the beginning to back her initial impulse with twelve or fourteen more divisions drawn from the vanished Russian front, is an inquiry which may well occupy and instruct the military student. But Ludendorff was nursing other plans, larger, more ambitious and as it turned out fatal to his country. Already the vast design of the German offensive in 1918 had gripped his mind. Italy was but a 'side show,' worth perhaps 'the bones of a Pomeranian Grenadier,' but never to obstruct a classical theory and the supreme trial of strength against the strongest foe. Yet the falling away of Italy, a people of

40 millions, a first-class power, from the cause of the Allies at this time would have been an event more pregnant with consequences than all the triumphs of March 21, 1918. To overwhelm Italy and to sue for a general peace afforded still the surest hope for the Central Empires. It is a valid though inadequate claim on the part of the British High Command that the continuous pressure on Paschendale played its part in influencing the German war mind. The almost inexhaustible resources of the British attack, its conquering of superhuman difficulties, its obstinate Commanders, its undaunted troops, the repeated destruction of the German front lines, the drain—half ours, but still frightful—on German resources, all riveted the eyes of Ludendorff on the Western Front. God forbid that such sacrifices, however needless, however disproportioned, should be vain!

From these deep matters I must recall the reader to the limited situation from which my tale is told.

It was imperative that Italy should be rearmed to the utmost possible extent by France and England. On November 18 I proceeded to Paris to meet in conclave with Loucheur and the Italian Minister of Armaments, General Dallolio. It was a cheerless experience; our margins were so small, our needs so exacting—and the Italian void gaped. In those hard days defeat was not leniently viewed by overstrained Allies. We all went through it in our turn—the politeness which veiled depreciation, the sympathy which scarcely surmounted resentment. And here I must pay my tribute to the dignity and quiet courage of the Italian Minister, and to the respect which in such circumstances he knew how to command from all.

Mr. Churchill to Prime Minister and Lord Derby.

November 21, 1917.

General Furse and I have after consultation to-day met first Loucheur and secondly Loucheur and Dallolio. We have arranged as follows: (1) The French will send at once 150,000 rifles, complete transportation of which will begin to-night and take about eight days. We shall give an equal number beginning on the ninth day with possibility of some delay in the latter portion. (2) The French will give 2,000 mitrailleuses and we 2,000 hotchkiss guns spread over next few weeks. (3) Ammunition as requested for all the above from both French and British sources. (4) French will give immediately 300 field guns ('seventy-fives') with ammunition. We reserved our undertaking on this item on account of the difficulty, though Italians requested 300 field guns from us. The 15-pounders may afford a partial solution. (5) French will give from 175 to 200 medium guns and howitzers with ammunition. We have promised to do our best to provide up to 175 of various medium natures, but we have warned the Italians that possibly the whole number cannot be found. It is understood that these deliveries will be spread over two months. (6) French cannot give any heavy or very heavy pieces, but we have undertaken to give 40 heavy—probably 8-inch howitzers with ammunition—which is Italian total demand. (7) We have refused very heavy natures. (8) We have stated that we consider 40 tanks if sent at all should be complete with British personnel and as part of British force and that this is a matter for General Staff. Above appears to be upon the whole satisfactory arrangement to meet the emergency. In making it we have kept in view possibility that it may be better to supply the deficiency in field guns and medium natures by increasing the proportion of organised artillery batteries with British force rather than by sending unfamiliar equipments to the Italian army which we need ourselves. General Furse leaves for London to-night. I return the day after.

Secondly Loucheur will endeavour to secure a rebate of 250,000 tons out of 2,000,000 allocated to France and Italy for food in aid of my promised deliveries of steel to him. If he fails I am free to review the position within these limits.

*   *   *   *   *

The Paschendale offensive had ended in mire and carnage, when suddenly there emerged from the British sector opposite Cambrai a battle totally different in character from any yet fought in the war. For the first time the mechanical method of securing Surprise was effectively used. Boraston's account points to this battle as a refutation of 'the crude talk about the backward method of our leadership in France during 1916–17; its lack of genius or skill; its prodigious waste of life.'[1] Here in his opinion was a superb example of scientific novelty and audacious tactics combined into a conception of military genius. But this conception, not only its underlying idea but its methods and even its instruments, had been pressed upon the British High Command for almost exactly two years. The plan of attack at Cambrai was inherent in the original conception of the Tank. It was for this, and for this precisely, that Tanks had been devised. In my first memorandum on armoured Caterpillar vehicles, written for Sir John French on December 3, 1915, the following passages occurred:—

'The cutting of the enemy's wire and the general domination of his firing-line can be effected by engines of this character. About seventy are now nearing completion in England, and should be inspected. None should be used until all can be used at once. They should be disposed secretly along the whole attacking front two or three hundred yards apart. Ten or fifteen minutes before the assault these engines should move forward over the best line of advance open, passing through or across our trenches at prepared points. They are capable of traversing any ordinary obstacle, ditch, breastwork, or trench. They carry two or three Maxims each, and can be fitted with flame apparatus. Nothing but a direct hit from a field gun will stop them. On reaching the enemy's wire they turn to the left or right and run down parallel to the enemy's trench, sweeping his parapet with their fire, and crushing and cutting the barbed wire in lanes and in a slightly serpentine course. . . .

'If artillery is used to cut wire, the direction and imminence of the attack is proclaimed days beforehand. But by this method the assault follows the wire-cutting almost immediately, *i.e.* before any reinforcements can be brought up by the enemy, or any special defensive measure taken.

[1] *Sir Douglas Haig's Command*, Vol. I, Ch. XV, p. 283.

'The Caterpillars are capable of actually crossing the enemy's trench and advancing to cut his communication trenches; but into this aspect it is not necessary to go now. One step at a time. It will be easy, when the enemy's front line is in our hands, to find the best places for the Caterpillars to cross by for any further advance which may be required. They can climb any slope. They are, in short, movable machine-gun cupolas as well as wire-smashers. . . .

'Surprise consists in novelty and suddenness. Secrecy is vital, and it would be possible, over a period of three or four weeks, to work routine conditions into such a state that very little extraordinary preparation would be required. The weak man-power available in the enemy's front line can easily be overwhelmed by forces which might appear to be assembled in the ordinary course.'

These words in a paper printed by the Committee of Imperial Defence had been read by Sir Douglas Haig before the end of 1915.[1] Tanks in considerable and growing numbers had been in action on the British front since their conception had been improvidently exposed to the enemy on the Somme in 1916. At the Headquarters of the Tank Corps the original tactical ideas inspiring their conception had been earnestly and thoroughly developed. The Tank Corps had never yet been allowed to put them into practice. These engines had been used in small numbers as mere ancillaries to infantry and artillery battles. They had been condemned to wallow in the crater fields under the full blast of massed German artillery, or to founder in the mud of Paschendale. Never had they been allowed to have their own chance in a battle made for them, adapted to their special capacities, and in which they could render the inestimable service for which they had been specially designed.

The success of a few Tanks in a minor operation at Paschendale, where in the Army Corps of General Maxse they

[1] See also my reference to Tank tactics in the Memorandum of Oct. 21, 1917, of which a print had been sent to G.H.Q.

were correctly employed, was probably the means of rescuing the Tank Corps from the increasing disfavour into which their engines had fallen through being so long mishandled by the British Headquarters. Whatever may have been the reason, the fact remains that 'a project which had been constantly in the mind of the General Staff of the Tank Corps for nearly three months and in anticipation of which preparations had already been undertaken, was approved, and its date fixed for November 20.' [1] All the requisite conditions were at last accorded. The Tanks were to operate on ground not yet ploughed up by artillery, against a front not yet prepared to meet an offensive. Above all, Surprise! The Tanks were themselves to open the attack. With a daring acceptance of responsibility Sir Julian Byng, who commanded the Army, ordered that not a shot was to be fired by the British artillery, not even for registration, until the Tanks were actually launched. The Artillery schemes which for the first time rendered this feat practicable without mishap to the troops reflect the highest credit on their authors.

The minutely prepared scheme of the Tank Corps had the following aim:—'To effect the penetration of four systems of trenches in a few hours without any type of artillery preparation.' [2] Nearly 500 Tanks were available. 'To-morrow,' write General Elles, Commander of the Tank Corps, in his Special Order to his men, 'the Tank Corps will have the chance for which it has been waiting for many months—to operate on good going in the van of the battle.'

'The attack,' says the historian of the Tank Corps (Colonel Fuller), 'was a stupendous success. As the Tanks moved forward with the infantry following close behind, the enemy completely lost his balance, and those who did not fly panic-stricken from the field surrendered with little or no resistance. . . . By 4 p.m. on November 20 one of the most astonishing battles

[1] Colonel Fuller, *Tanks in the Great War*, Chapter XIX, p. 140.
[2] *Ibid.*, p. 141.

in all history had been won and, as far as the Tank Corps was concerned, tactically finished, for no reserves existing it was not possible to do more.'[1] In the brief life of a November day the whole German trench system had been penetrated

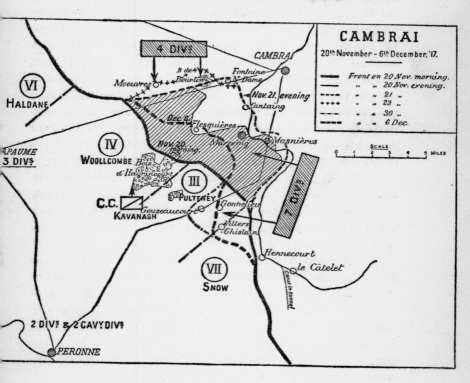

on a front of 6 miles, and 10,000 prisoners and 200 guns captured, without the loss of more than 1,500 British soldiers. 'It is a question,' declares the Staff Officer, 'whether any stroke of the allied army on the Western Front was more fruitful ultimately of ground and result than this battle of Cambrai, despite its limited design.'[2]

[1] *Ibid.*, pp. 148, 150.   [2] *Sir Douglas Haig's Command*, p. 392.

But if this was so, why not have done it before? Why not have done it on a far larger scale? If British and French war leaders had possessed—not more genius, for the possibilities had by this time been obvious to all who were studying the Tank problem—but the vision and comprehension which is expected from the honoured chiefs of great armies, there was no reason why a battle like Cambrai could not have been fought a year before, or better still, why three or four concerted battles like Cambrai could not have been fought simultaneously in the spring of 1917. Then indeed the enemy's front line pierced at once in three or four places might have been completely overwhelmed on a front of 50 miles. Then indeed the roll forward of the whole army might have been achieved and the hideous deadlock broken.

But, it will be said, such assertions take insufficient account of the practical difficulties, of the slowly gathered experience, of the immense refinements of study, discipline and organisation required. Could, for instance, 3,000 Tanks have been manufactured by the spring of 1917? Could the men to handle them have been spared from the front? Could their tactical training have been perfected behind the line and out of contact with the enemy? Could the secret have been kept? Would not preparation on so large a scale, even behind the line, have become apparent to the enemy? To all these questions we will answer that one-tenth of the mental effort expended by the Headquarters Staff on preparing the old-fashioned offensives of which the war had consisted, one-twentieth of the influence they used to compel reluctant Governments to sanction these offensives, one-hundredth of the men lost in them, would have solved all the problems easily and overwhelmingly before the spring of 1917. As for the Germans getting to hear of it, learning, for instance, that the British were practising with Caterpillar armoured cars at dummy trenches behind their lines on a large scale—what use would they have made of their knowledge? What use did

Ludendorff make of the awful disclosure, not as a mere rumour or questionable Intelligence report, but of the actual apparition of the Tanks in September, 1916? There is a melancholy comfort in reflecting that if the British and French commands were short-sighted, the ablest soldier in Germany was blind. In truth these high military experts all belong to the same school. Haig at least moved faster and farther along the new path, and in consequence, doubtingly and tardily, he reaped in the end a generous reward.

It has been necessary to the whole argument of this volume to dwell insistently upon these aspects of the Battle of Cambrai. Accusing as I do without exception all the great ally offensives of 1915, 1916, and 1917, as needless and wrongly conceived operations of infinite cost, I am bound to reply to the question, What else could be done? And I answer it, pointing to the Battle of Cambrai, '*This* could have been done.' This in many variants, this in larger and better forms ought to have been done, and would have been done if only the Generals had not been content to fight machine-gun bullets with the breasts of gallant men, and think that that was waging war.

It remains only to be said of the Battle of Cambrai that the initial success so far exceeded the expectations of the Third Army Staff that no suitable preparations had been made to exploit it. The Cavalry who scampered forward were naturally soon held up by snipers and machine guns, and no important advance beyond the first day's gains was achieved. The railways at this part of the German front favoured a rapid hostile concentration, and ten days after the victory the Germans delivered a most powerful counter-stroke in which they recaptured a large portion of the conquered ground and took in their turn 10,000 prisoners and 200 guns. In this counter-attack the enemy used for the first time those tactics of 'infiltration' by small highly competent parties of machine-gunners or trench-mortar men, which they were soon to employ on a larger scale. The bells which had been rung for

Cambrai were therefore judged premature, and the year 1917 closed on the allied fronts, British, French, Italian, Russian and Balkan, in a gloom relieved only by Allenby's sword-flash at Jerusalem.

CHAPTER XV

BRITAIN CONQUERS THE U–BOATS

'Depend upon it, Sir, when a man knows he is to be hanged in a fortnight, it concentrates his mind wonderfully.'

[*Dr. Johnson.*]

'Nearly succeeded'—The Fatal Puzzle—The Anatomy of the Submarine—Surface or Submerged Attack—Arming of the Mercantile Marine—The Q-ships—The Episode of the *Dunraven*—The German Dilemma—Depth Charges and Destroyers—Detector Nets—The Prelude to Unrestricted Warfare—The Crisis of the Struggle—Admiralty Counter-measures—The Question of Convoy: pros and cons—My March Memorandum—Wireless Control of Shipping—Importance of Concentration both of Shipping and Protection—Carson's anxious tenure—Triumph of the Convoy System—The Dover Barrage—Admiral Keyes in Command—The Giant Anglo-American Barrage—The Hunters hunted—Total Defeat of the U-boat—The Price

IT is commonly said that the German drive on Paris in 1914 and the unlimited U-boat warfare both 'nearly succeeded.' But this expression requires analysis, and also differentiation between the issues on land and sea. A partisan watching an evenly contested football match, an engineer watching a vehicle whose weight he does not know exactly, crossing a bridge whose strength he has never been able to measure, experiences no doubt similar sensations of anxiety or excitement. The processes however are different. A football match like a great battle on land is in a continual state of flux and chance. But whether the vehicle will break down the bridge does not depend on chance. It depends on the weight of the vehicle and the strength of the bridge. When both these are unknown beforehand, anxiety is natural. But once it is known that the bridge will bear at least ten tons and the vehicle at the most weighs no more than eight, all misgivings are proved to have been unfounded. To say that the vehicle 'nearly' broke down the bridge is untrue. There was never any chance of it. Whereas any one of a score of alternative accidents would have given the German Army Paris in 1914, the seafaring resources of Great Britain were in fact and in the circumstances always superior to the U-boat attack. Moreover that attack was inherently of a character so gradual that these superior resources could certainly obtain their full development.

Nevertheless, the struggle between the British sailormen, Royal and Mercantile—for both played an equally indispensable part—and the German U-boats stands among the most heart-shaking episodes of history, and its declared result will for generations be regarded as a turning point in the destiny of nations. It was in scale and in stake the greatest conflict ever decided at sea. It was almost entirely a duel between Britain and Germany. Austrian submarines assisted the Germans. Allied navies, United States and Japanese destroyers, helped Great Britain to the best of their power. But three-quarters of the tonnage sunk was British, and 175 U-boats out of a total German war loss of 182 were destroyed by British agency.

The shortcomings in the higher command of the British Navy, afloat and at home, which had led to Admiral de Robeck's failure to force the Dardanelles, to the abortive conclusion of Jutland, and to the neglect to carry the fighting into the German Bight, had given to the enemy during 1915 and 1916 the means of developing an entirely novel form of sea attack upon a scale the potential intensity of which no one could measure beforehand, and which if successful would be fatal. At first sight all seemed to favour the challengers. Two hundred U-boats each possessing between three and four weeks' radius of action, each capable of sinking with torpedo, gun fire or bomb four or five vessels in a single day, beset the approaches to an island along which there passed in and out every week several thousand merchant vessels. The submarine, with only a periscope showing momentarily like a broomstick above the waves, could discharge its torpedo unseen. It could rise to the surface and fire its gun to sink, burn or induce the surrender of a defenceless vessel, and disappear into the invisible depths of the vast waste of water without leaving a trace behind. Of all the tasks ever set to a Navy none could have appeared more baffling than that of sheltering this enormous traffic and groping deep below the surface of the sea for the deadly elusive foe. It was in fact a game of blind man's buff in an unlimited space of three dimensions.

Had the problem been surveyed in cold blood beforehand it might well have seemed insoluble. But in the event as the danger grew, so grew also the will power of the threatened State and the courage, endurance and ingenuity of its servants. At the summit through the authority of the Prime Minister all misgivings were suppressed, all croakers silenced, and all doubters banished from executive responsibility. But strict inquiry was made into facts, and no official grimace passed long for argument. The qualities of audacity, initiative and seamanship inbred in the sailors and younger officers of the Navy found in this new warfare their highest opportunity. But without the unquenchable spirit of the Merchant Service nothing would have availed. The foundation of all defence lay in the fact that Merchant-seamen three or four times 'submarined' returned unfalteringly to the perilous seas, and even in the awful month when one ship out of every four that left the United Kingdom never came home, no voyage was delayed for lack of resolute civilian volunteers.

To realise the issues of this strange form of warfare hitherto unknown to human experience, the reader must understand the general anatomy of the submarine. This delicate vessel is driven when on the surface by powerful oil engines which in those days yielded speeds up to sixteen or seventeen knots an hour. Submerged she depended upon electric accumulators which she could recharge by her oil engines when on the surface. These accumulators produced a maximum speed under water of about eight knots, and would last about one hour at full and twenty at economical speed. In order to dive, a submarine does not give herself negative buoyancy, *i.e.* make herself heavier than the water. She fills enough tanks to have about a ton of buoyancy in hand and then, by depressing her horizontal rudders and going ahead on her electric motors, swims down to the desired depth. A submarine is strong enough to resist the ever-increasing water pressures down to about two hundred and fifty feet below the surface. Beyond that depth there is increasing risk of leakage through the joints of her hull. Any serious penetration by salt water may liberate chlorine gas from the electric accumulators and choke the crew in tortures. Beyond a depth of three or four hundred feet a submarine would certainly be destroyed by the water pressure and would swiftly sink bilged to the ocean floor. In deep water therefore a submarine could only remain submerged while in motion, and could only keep in motion as long as her accumulators lasted. When these were exhausted, she must come to the surface and float defenceless during several hours while they were being recharged. On the other hand, where the sea was not more than two hundred and fifty feet deep, a submarine need not fear to give herself negative buoyancy. She could sink and sit on the bottom without using up her accumulators as long as the air and oxygen tubes she carried enabled the crew to breathe. This allowed her to remain below water for at least forty-eight hours, during which time she could also move perhaps sixty miles. The power to remain submerged for more than twenty hours was thus limited to the shallow seas. On the other hand, depths of less than fifty feet raised difficulties of another kind which prevented submerged attacks.

The prime weapon of all submarines was the torpedo;

and as long as they fought warships, no other weapon was of any service. Thin-skinned submersible vessels could only engage in an artillery duel with armoured surface ships at a fatal disparity in risk. The penetration of a U-boat's hull by a single shot deprived her of the power of diving, even if it did not sink her outright. But when the Germans decided to use their U-boats to attack merchant ships, another set of arguments arose. The merchant ships were so numerous that the torpedo was an unsuitable weapon for procuring decisive results. It was expensive, difficult and lengthy to manufacture; the supply could only gradually be broadened out; and only from eight to twenty torpedoes could be carried in submarines according to their classes. As a large proportion of torpedoes missed their target for one fault or another, the destructive power of a U-boat against commerce during a single cruise was severely limited. Therefore the first move of the Germans was to arm their U-boats with guns to attack merchant ships on the surface of the water, sinking them either by gun fire or, after surrender, by bombs placed on board.

This method also enabled the U-boats to use their much superior surface speed, and allowed them to discriminate between different classes of merchant ships and between enemy and neutral ships; to observe their own Prize Law by visit and search; and finally to give time for the merchant crews, if they chose to surrender their vessel, to escape in open boats.

The first British counter-move, made on my responsibility in 1915, was to arm British merchantmen to the greatest possible extent with guns of sufficient power to deter the U-boat from surface attack. When this was achieved, the reduction of the assailant's speed and the limited torpedo supply increased the merchant ship's chance of escape proportionately. The argument was overwhelming. Unhappily there were at first hardly any guns either for merchant ships or for the coastal patrols. We searched every quarter of the globe and all the recesses of the Admiralty for guns, no matter how obsolete or various in pattern. A hundred coastal vessels by the spring of 1915 were provided with one 12-pounder gun apiece. The more important sea-going vessels were also armed. The scarcity was such that their guns had to be transferred from outward- to inward-bound vessels at ports outside the submarine zone, so as to make them go further. Despite every effort made by my successor, Mr. Balfour, the supply of guns expanded slowly; and it was not until the autumn of 1916 that he was in a position to undertake the arming of the whole of the Mercantile Marine. Good progress had however been made before the submarine danger renewed itself in its gravest form.

As the U-boats were forced by the progressive arming of the British Mercantile Marine to rely increasingly on under-water attacks, they encountered a new set of dangers. The submerged U-boat with its defective vision ran the greatest risk of mistaking neutral for British vessels and of drowning neutral crews, and thus of embroiling Germany with other great Powers. We also resorted to the well-known *ruse de guerre* of hoisting false colours in order further to baffle and confuse the enemy. Thus from a very early stage the U-boats were forced to choose between all the practical inconveniences and far-reaching diplomatic consequences of under-water attack with the torpedo, or on the other hand facing the disproportionate hazards of the gun duel on the surface. It was at this stage that we developed the stratagem of the Q-ship. A number of merchant vessels were specially equipped with torpedo tubes and with concealed guns firing from behind trap-door bulwarks, and sent along the trade routes to offer themselves to the hostile submarines. When the U-boat, wishing to economise torpedoes, attacked the Q-ship by gun fire on the surface, a portion of the British crew took to the boats and by every device endeavoured to entice the Germans to close quarters. Once the enemy was within decisive range, the White Ensign was hoisted, the trap-doors fell and a deadly fire by trained gunners was opened upon them. By these means in 1915 and 1916 eleven U-boats were destroyed and the rest, rendered far more nervous of attacking by gun fire, were thrown back more and more upon their torpedoes. By the end of 1917 this process was complete. The German submarine commanders would not face the unequal gun-fire combat. The stratagem of the Q-ship was thus exhausted, and its last victim U.88 perished in September, 1917.

*   *   *   *   *

The action between the Q-ship *Dunraven* and U.61 affords a vivid example of this strange form of war. On the morning of August 8, 1917, H.M.S. *Dunraven*, disguised as an armed British merchant ship, was zigzagging towards the Bristol Channel, offering herself to submarine attack. At 10.58 a U-boat was sighted on the horizon two points before the starboard beam. The *Dunraven* continued to zigzag; and the U-boat, having approached submerged, broke surface at 11.43 on the starboard quarter and opened fire at about 5,000 yards. The *Dunraven*, playing her part as an armed merchantman, at once opened fire with her after gun (a 2½ pounder). Her Captain, Commander Gordon Campbell, ordered much smoke to be made from the funnels, but at the same time reduced speed to seven knots with an occasional zigzag to give the enemy a chance of closing. This the enemy did, and by 12.25 was scarcely a half-mile away. Meanwhile the *Dunraven's* unconcealed stern gun was intentionally firing short, and her Commander made *en clair* signals to deceive the U-boat, such as: 'Submarine chasing and shelling me'; 'Submarine overtaking me. Help. Come quickly'; 'Submarine (position). Am abandoning ship.' At 12.40, when the U-boat shells were falling near, Commander Campbell made a cloud of steam to pretend boiler trouble, and gave the order 'Abandon ship.' The *Dunraven* stopped, blowing off steam, and turned her broadside so that the enemy could see the panic on board. The crew tumbled into the boats, one of which purposely was left hanging by her after davit. Thus encouraged, U.61 closed warily and continued firing. A shell went through the poop, exploding a depth charge and blowing up a Lieutenant. Two more shells crashed into the poop, setting it on fire. Clouds of dense smoke poured from the burning vessel, partially hiding from view the now swiftly approaching U-boat. The magazine and also the store of depth charges of the *Dunraven* being in the poop, it was obvious that an explosion must soon take place. The crew of the secret 4-inch gun immediately above the magazine stood to their post, waiting in grim anxiety for an opportunity which they were not destined to see. U.61 was now 'coming along nicely from port to starboard to pass 400 or 500 yards off.' In a few minutes the attacker would be on the weather side and a perfect target. Commander Campbell therefore had the option of opening fire under difficult conditions or of waiting longer for a far better chance. He waited.

At 12.58, when the U-boat was passing close astern of the *Dunraven*, two depth charges and some cordite exploded. The 4-inch gun and the gun's crew were blown into the air. The gun itself was hurled onto the well deck, and the crew fell in various places—one man in the water amid a shower of scattered 4-inch ammunition. The 'open fire' buzzers of all the concealed guns were started by the explosion, and the gun on the after bridge (the only one bearing) opened fire. Had this misfortune been delayed for two minutes more, three guns could have fired on U.61 at 400 yards' range. U.61, warned from the size of the explosion that it had a Q-ship to deal with, dived instantly. Commander Campbell, realising that he was now about to be torpedoed, ordered the doctor to remove all the wounded and lock them up in the cabins, 'so as not to spoil the next part.' The fire hoses were turned on to the poop, which was a mass of flames. Although the deck was red hot, the magazine itself had not yet exploded. Meanwhile a warship had answered the *Dunraven's en clair* appeals for assistance, and fearing lest the action should be prematurely ended by her arrival, Commander Campbell signalled to her to keep away.

At 1.20 a torpedo was seen approaching from the starboard side. It struck abaft the engine room. The ruse of abandoning ship had already been exhausted so far as 'an armed merchant ship' was concerned. But the desperate condition of the *Dunraven* favoured the hope that it might succeed in another form. There is a moment when even a warship must be abandoned. The order was therefore given, 'Q abandon ship.' The two secret guns which had been exposed were left visible, and an additional party of men were ordered to escape by a raft and a damaged boat.

U.61 was now in great doubt. Was the ship finally abandoned or not? For nearly an hour, showing only his periscope, the submarine circled round the heeling, burning ship at various ranges. During this period boxes of cordite and 4-inch shells were continually exploding in the flames. At 2.30 U.61 broke surface directly astern, where no gun was bearing, and at a few hundred yards shelled the stricken ship. Nearly all the shells either hit the *Dunraven* or fell close to the boats, on which U.61 also fired with a Maxim. Two shells burst on the bridge with serious effects. All this time Commander Campbell still waited for a favourable chance.

At 2.50, U.61 ceased shelling, submerged, and steamed past the *Dunraven's* port side at about 150 yards' distance. Only a small part of the periscope was showing, but this revealed both depth and position. The long-awaited moment had now come. The *Dunraven* was armed not only with guns but with under-water torpedo tubes. Unfortunately she was heeling over so far that accurate aiming was spoiled. At 2.55 Commander Campbell fired a torpedo. The bubbles passed just ahead of the periscope; and the U-boat, unaware that destruction had missed her by a few inches, came slowly round onto the starboard side. This gave the *Dunraven* a second chance, and at 3.20 another torpedo was fired. Again the bubbles passed close to the periscope, and the deadly weapon can only have missed its mark by the narrowest margin. This time U.61 saw the peril and dived deep. Commander Campbell, having exhausted every device and with his ship in a sinking condition, signalled for assistance. Men-of-war, headed by the United States destroyer *Noma*, arrived from all quarters. The U-boat, whose periscope had again been seen, was hunted; and the *Dunraven*, after her crew had been rescued, foundered in the great approach route she had so faithfully defended. For his tireless perseverance in this action Commander Campbell received the Victoria Cross.

*   *   *   *   *

By all these manœuvres and pressures the Germans were confronted during 1916 with the dilemma either of losing a great many U-boats in gun duels or Q-ship ambuscades, or of resorting almost entirely to the torpedo with a vastly increased risk of offending neutrals. This complicated and nicely balanced discussion produced great stresses and cross-purposes between the German naval and civil authorities. The Naval Staff, headed by Tirpitz and Scheer, demanded that the authorities should sink at sight all vessels in the war zone. The Emperor and the Chancellor in their fear of offending neutrals insisted that the custom of visit and search should be complied with in the case of unarmed ships. But—protested the Naval Staff—which were the unarmed ships, and what would happen to the U-boat while she was making her inquiries? They declared moreover that unrestricted warfare would increase the sinkings to such an extent that Britain would be forced within six months to sue for peace.

The relative vulnerability of armed and unarmed ships can be judged from the following summary of U-boat attacks on British vessels between January 1, 1916 and January 25, 1917.

	Defensively armed ships.	Unarmed ships.
Number attacked	310	302
Sunk by torpedoes without warning .	62	30
Sunk by gun fire or bombs . . .	12	205
Escaped	236	67
Percentage escaped	76	22

These figures are illuminating and conclusive. They show that the U-boat was scarcely ever willing to face the gun duel with an armed vessel; and in consequence that with equal number of ships attacked the armed ship had nearly four times the unarmed ship's chance of escape. So much for the first great measure of defence.

* * * * *

The principal means of *attacking* submarines under water was by dropping overboard charges which exploded at a certain depth. The shock of these explosions seriously jarred the submarine, and if near enough, deranged her mechanism or opened her joints. These depth charges were our earliest anti-submarine device. Gradually the methods of dropping them improved, and their size and number were multiplied many times. The arch-enemy of the submarine was the destroyer. She had the fastest speed, the greatest number of depth charges, and was herself cheaper than the quarry she hunted. When the periscope of a U-boat was seen in deep water all the available destroyers and motor launches and other fast small craft spread in an organised network over the surface so as to keep her down and force her to exhaust her accumulators; and alike in deep water or in shallow, the slightest indication of her whereabouts—an air bubble, an oil stain on the surface—drew the dreaded depth charges in a searching shower. As the struggle progressed the skill and methods of the hunting vessel perpetually improved. Wonderful instruments were devised for detecting the beat of a submarine propeller; and with this and other indications a U-boat was sometimes pursued to death after an intermittent but unrelenting chase of more than thirty-six hours, during which the U-boat perhaps replenished her electric batteries on the surface unseen two or three times.

The second anti-submarine weapon was the thin wire net hung in long strips across straits or narrow channels. These nets, buoyed on the surface with glass balls, were intended to foul the propeller of the U-boat and to cling about the hull. A U-boat thus enveloped, even if her motive power was not affected, would unconsciously be trailing a fatal tell-tale buoy about upon the surface, thus guiding her pursuers. To these light nets there were added in particular channels elaborately devised necklaces of mines joined with nets and watched by large numbers of trawlers with destroyers at ready call. Collision was another danger for this slow-moving, half-blind creature; and the ram of battleship, cruiser, destroyer or merchant ship on frequent occasions exacted the final forfeit.

Lastly, submarines stalked one another, and a U-boat while attacking a merchant ship or recharging its batteries upon the surface was on more than one occasion blown to pieces by the torpedo of a submerged pursuer of whose approach she was unconscious. The brutal features inseparable from the submarine attack on merchant vessels, and the miserable fate which so often overtook the passengers and civilian crew, inspired this warfare with exceptional fierceness. The attack upon warships, however grievous in loss of life, was considered fair war by the Royal Navy. The sinking of merchant vessels or neutral ships or hospital ships seemed to be a barbarous, treacherous and piratical act deserving every conceivable means of extermination. When we consider that nearly thirteen thousand British lives were destroyed by the German U-boats and that many were civilians, and the cruel

and shocking incidents—to some extent inevitable—which characterized this warfare, and when we remember further the awful character of the stakes, the fact that several hundred German officers and men were rescued from the sea or allowed to surrender after scuttling their vessels is a tribute to the restraint of the deeply injured conqueror.

The Germans had originally decided to begin unrestricted submarine war on April 1, 1916. The threat of the United States to break off relations after the attack on the *Sussex* led at the end of the month to the permission being withdrawn. When Admiral Scheer, an ardent advocate of unrestricted warfare, received this order he intemperately recalled the High Sea fleet U-boats, refusing to permit them to work on the basis of visit and search. From May to October therefore the campaign was practically confined to the Mediterranean and to the mine-layers of the Flanders flotilla. The relief thus afforded to Great Britain in northern waters was however both fleeting and illusory. The Mediterranean U-boats, working in accordance with German prize procedure, succeeded in sinking a large number of ships, and the German Naval Staff on October 6 ordered Scheer to resume restricted warfare with the North Sea flotillas. In the interval the number of U-boats available for active service had risen from 47 in March to 93 in November. The sinkings consequently increased rapidly when operations were resumed. The average monthly loss for the period April to September had been 131,000 tons; that from November to February rose to 276,000 tons. By the end of 1916 it was evident that the development of anti-submarine measures had not kept pace with the increasing intensity of the attack. The defensive measures instituted during 1915 had increased the number of armed merchantmen and auxiliary patrol vessels, but the problem of actually attacking and destroying U-boats was still in a rudimentary stage.

On February 1 the unrestricted attack began in full vigour,

and the numbers of the U-boats continually increased. The losses of British, Allied and neutral vessels increased from 181 in January to 259 in February, 325 in March, and 423 in April; the corresponding figures in gross tonnage being 298,000 in January, 468,000 in February, 500,000 in March, and 849,000 in April. We now know that the German Naval Staff estimated that British shipping could be reduced at a rate of 600,000 tons a month, and that in five months at this rate Britain would be forced to her knees. In April alone the total world tonnage lost reached the appalling figure of 849,000 tons. The average monthly loss of British shipping during April, May and June from U-boats amounted to 409,-300 tons, corresponding to a rate of nearly five million tons a year. By the end of May, apart from vessels employed on naval and military services on essential trade in distant waters, and undergoing repairs, there was less than six million tons of shipping available for all the supplies and trade with the United Kingdom. If losses continued at this rate and were equally divided among the services exposed to attack, the tonnage available for trade at the beginning of 1918 would be reduced to under five million tons, that is to say, an amount almost exactly equal to the gross sinkings in 1917. It seemed that Time, hitherto counted as an incorruptible Ally, was about to change sides.

Nor did the entry of the United States into the war shed any beam of hope on these dark waters. The longed-for American resources required a vast array of British tonnage to transport them to the Front. The patrol system in the approaches to the English Channel and South of Ireland had completely broken down. Not only were the limited numbers of the patrol vessels unable to protect the shipping, but their mere presence assisted the submarines to find the traffic routes. In April the great approach route to the south-west of Ireland was becoming a veritable cemetery of British shipping, in which large vessels were sunk regularly day by

COMPARISON BETWEEN NUMBERS OF GERMAN SUBMARINES DESTROYED BY DIFFERENT TYPES OF SHIPS.

AUXILIARY PATROL. (Trawlers, Drifters etc.) — 37

DESTROYERS. — 31

SUBMARINES. — 17

"Q" SHIPS. — 11

AIRCRAFT. — 7

MERCHANT SHIPS. — 5

CRUISERS. — 3

BATTLESHIPS. — 1

COMPARISON BETWEEN THE PRINCIPAL WEAPONS OF DESTRUCTION.

MINES. — 42

DEPTH CHARGES. — 31

GUNFIRE. — 30

RAM. — 19

TORPEDO. — 17

BLOWN UP BY GERMANS. (To avoid capture) — 14

WRECKS AND ACCIDENTS. — 10

MINE NETS. — 7

INTERNED. — 7

SWEEPS ETC. — 3

COMPARISON BETWEEN NUMBERS OF GERMAN SUBMARINES DESTROYED BY GREAT BRITAIN AND HER ALLIES.

TOTAL GERMAN SUBMARINE LOSSES.............199

TOTAL DESTROYED BY THE BRITISH NAVY........175
(Including number blown up to avoid capture)

TOTAL DESTROYED BY THE FRENCH NAVY.........3

"   "   "   " U.S.A.   " 2

"   "   "   " RUSSIAN " 2

Data compiled from British and German sources

day about 200 miles from land. During this month it was calculated that one in four merchant ships leaving the United Kingdom never returned. The U-boat was rapidly undermining not only the life of the British islands, but the foundations of the Allies' strength; and the danger of their collapse in 1918 began to loom black and imminent.

The stern pressure of events reacted upon Admiralty organisation. In May the Naval Staff was given an appropriate position on the Board by the merging of the office of First Sea Lord and Chief of Staff, while the addition of a Deputy and Assistant who could each act with Board authority accelerated business and relieved the Chief of Staff of a mass of work. The Operations Division, hitherto troubled like Martha over many things, had not been able to think far enough ahead. In May a small planning section was instituted, charged with the study of policy and preparation of plans; and this was later in the year expanded into a separate Division. Younger officers were called to the Admiralty and more responsibility was given to them. Without this reorganisation of the Staff, the measures that defeated the U-boat, even if conceived, could not have been executed. These measures took a threefold form: first, the preparation and launching of extensive mining plans; secondly, the further development of research and supply in the technical fields of mines, depth charges and hydrophones; and thirdly, the decisive step, the institution of a convoy system which involved the escort and control of all merchant shipping.

I had instituted the convoy system for troopships crossing the oceans at the beginning of the war. Then the attack by faster German light cruisers was the danger. The guns of an obsolete battleship or heavy cruiser could certainly drive away any hostile raiders then loose upon the surface of the seas. We had also from the beginning used destroyer escorts to convoy troopships in and out through the submarine zone. In no case did any mishap occur. It did not however seem reasonable to expect similar results from the convoy system in the case of attack by submarines upon merchant ships. On the contrary it seemed obvious that hostile submarines would work more damage in the midst of a crowd of merchantmen than against isolated vessels; and it was further evident that the escorting warships would themselves be among the targets of the enemy torpedoes. The U-boat attacks on trade in 1915 and the early part of 1916 seemed to have been confined within tolerable limits by the numbers of merchant vessels at sea, by the variety of their routes and ports, by the uncertainty of their times of arrival, and above all by the size of the sea. The system of watching and patrolling in the greatest strength possible the confluences of trade had worked well against the German raiding cruisers, and for the first two years of the war the Admiralty relied upon it against the U-boats without serious misadventure.

When under the pressure of ever-increasing losses the remedy of convoys was again advocated by the younger officers of the Admiralty War Staff, it encountered opposition from practically every quarter. Every squadron and every naval base was clamant for destroyers, and convoy meant taking from them even those that they had. There would be delays due to assembling. There must be reduction in speed of the faster vessels and congestion of ships in port. The scale and difficulties of the task were exaggerated, and it was argued that the larger the number of ships in company, the greater the risk from submarines. This convincing logic could only be refuted by the proof of facts. In January, 1917, the official Admiralty opinion was expressed as follows:

'A system of several ships sailing in company as a convoy is not recommended in any area where submarine attack is a possibility. It is evident that the larger the number of ships forming a convoy, the greater the chance of a submarine being able to attack successfully and the greater the difficulty of the escort in preventing such an attack.'

The French and United States naval authorities were also opposed to the convoy system, and at a Conference held in February, 1917, representative Masters of merchant ships took the same view.

Now let us see what was overlooked in this high, keen and earnest consensus. The size of the sea is so vast that the difference between the size of a convoy and the size of a single ship shrinks in comparison almost to insignificance. There was in fact very nearly as good a chance of a convoy of forty ships in close order slipping unperceived between the patrolling U-boats as there was for a single ship; and each time this happened, forty ships escaped instead of one. Here then was the key to the success of the convoy system against U-boats. The concentration of ships greatly reduced the number of targets in a given area and thus made it more difficult for the submarines to locate their prey. Moreover the convoys were easily controlled and could be quickly deflected by wireless from areas known to be dangerous at any given moment. Finally the destroyers, instead of being dissipated on patrol over wide areas, were concentrated at the point of the hostile attack, and opportunities of offensive action frequently arose. Thirteen U-boats were actually destroyed while endeavouring to molest convoys. This fear of instant retaliation from convoy escorts had a demoralising effect upon the enemy, and consequently U-boat attacks were not always pressed home.

Most of this was still unproved in the early days of 1917. There stood only the fact that troopship convoys had always been escorted through the submarine zones during 1915 and 1916 and had enjoyed complete immunity from attack. The highest professional opinion remained opposed to convoy as a defence against U-boats, and personally I rested under that impression. I had no official position at that time, but I had confidential relations with Ministers and was informed both upon the discussion and the facts. I therefore wrote in March for the First Lord of the Admiralty, Sir Edward Carson, the following note. It was intended to offer an alternative means of gaining the advantages claimed by its advocates for the convoy system without running counter to the solid objections of the naval authorities. I print it because it throws a contemporary light upon the problem and because, although the method proposed was rejected in favour of a simpler and more practical plan, the reasonings are sound.

March, 1917.

It is assumed for the purposes of this argument that the Germans use about fifty submarines at a time in three reliefs; that every submarine remains out about a month and takes (except in the case of the Zeebrugge boats) from two to three days to get to its beat.

The number of enemy submarines actually on the watch is not large enough to allow of any great concentration: they must be widely dispersed to cover the whole extended approaches to these islands. There cannot be any large number in any one station. The amount of damage which a submarine can do is limited by its store of torpedoes, and also by the hours of the day. Tackling even a single ship involves a considerable time. What a submarine wants in order to make its best bag is a steady trickle of shipping day after day more or less evenly dispersed along all the routes approaching these islands. It is arguable that *a greater concentration both of shipping and of the means of protection*, now here now there along particular routes and at particular times, would sensibly reduce the proportion of losses.

The measures suggested are as follows:—

Tell all ships which have wireless who are approaching our shores and expect to enter the area of submarine activity by nightfall—say Monday night—to steam back on their course for thirty-six hours and then to resume their voyage. Tell all ships who would similarly arrive on Tuesday night to steam back on their course for twenty-four hours; and all ships that would similarly arrive on Wednesday night to steam back on their course for twelve hours—and then in all cases resume their voyage. The result of this would be to create four blank days and to quadruple the volume of shipping arriving in the danger zone on the fourth day. For three days therefore the

German submarines would be useless and would find no prey. On the fourth day they would be confronted with a crowd of shipping out of which it is possible, owing to their limited numbers, that they could not take a proportionate toll. It is clear that you could afford to lose four times as much shipping on the fourth day as on any one of the four days without being worse off. If the number of submarines remains few and constant—their activity being in many respects a limited factor —while the volume of traffic is quadrupled, there is a very fair prospect of the proportion of losses not increasing in anything like the same ratio as the proportion of shipping. One knows that if you want a big bag of pheasants you beat them out of the cover in twos and threes, whereas if it is intended to shoot the cover over again the whole lot should be driven out as quickly as possible in the largest numbers. If rabbits run across a ride past a limited number of guns, their best chance is to run unexpectedly and all at once. It is quite possible that these simple analogies have a wider application. . . .

There is no reason to believe that losses are proportionate to the volume of traffic; the variations from day to day effectively prove this. There is every reason to believe that losses are limited by increased protection. The ships fitted with wireless are the most important and the largest; they are the ones which raise the tonnage totals. The experiment applied to them alone, as it necessarily must be, would be well worth while attempting. But if it were successful, the universal adoption of wireless in our merchant service would follow as a matter of course. . . .

The intermittence and uncertainty which may be imparted to the movements of our shipping by the regulation of *time* can be supplemented by the variation of *routes*. After one accumulation of shipping has been released upon (say) the Bristol Channel, the next might be directed on Liverpool or the Clyde—all the available protection being meanwhile concentrated so far as possible upon the route about to be used.

It fell to Sir Edward Carson's lot during his tenure as First Lord to face the most anxious and trying period of the naval war. During those eight months the U-boat sinkings of merchantmen reached their terrible climax. It was under his administration that the peak was surmounted and most of the important decisions of principle were taken by which the peril was ultimately overcome. The trial of the convoy system was urged upon the naval authorities by the Cabinet, and in this the Prime Minister took a decisive part.

At the end of April, 1917, the Director of the Anti-Submarine Division definitely advocated the introduction of convoys, and the first one left Gibraltar on May 10. It was entirely successful, and regular convoys commenced from the United States on June 4. Instructions were issued on June 22 to extend the system to Canadian ports, and on July 31 similar orders were issued for the South Atlantic trade. The entry of the United States facilitated convoys by opening her harbours as ports of assembly and by the precious aid of a number of her destroyers for escort work. More than a quarter of the whole of the escorts across the Atlantic were provided by American destroyers, and the comradeship of this hard service forms an ineffaceable tradition for the two navies.

The convoy organisation will for ever stand as a monument to the constancy and courage of the Royal Navy and Mercantile Marine. No credit is too high for the officers and men who without previous training navigated these fleets of forty or fifty ships in close formation through all the winds that blew. No service ever carried out by the Navy was of greater value to the State than that of the escort vessels. Those who have served in small ships will realise the skill, faithfulness and hardihood required to carry out this duty day after day, month after month, in wild weather and wintry seas without breakdown or failure. The control and arrangements of the Admiralty and the Ministry of Shipping became more thorough and perfect with every week that passed.

The convoy system was at first confined to homeward-bound vessels. The percentage of sinkings in the outward sailings at once began to rise. In August, 1917, convoy was extended to outward-bound vessels. The diagram on the opposite page reveals at a glance the triumph of convoy. By the end of October, 1917, 99 homeward convoys, comprising over 1,500 steamers of a deadweight capacity of 10,656,000 tons, had been brought in with the loss of only 10 ships torpedoed while actually in convoy, and of 14 which had become separated.

While convoy was vastly improving the protection of trade, all methods of attacking the U-boats were progressively developed, and the rate of destruction steadily rose. In April, 1917, British submarine flotillas were based upon Scapa Flow, Lough Swilly on the North, and Killybegs on the West coast of Ireland, and began to lie in wait for U-boats passing north-about to attack the great trade route. At the same time in the Southern part of the North Sea the small British 'C' Class submarines were released from harbour defence for the same duties. This method by which submarine vessels preyed on each other yielded substantial results. Seven U-boats were destroyed by it in 1917 and six in 1918. The threat of submarine attack also forced the U-boats to submerge much more frequently and for longer periods on their passage, with consequent delays in reaching their beats.

The mine however proved to be the most effective killing weapon. The Admiralty, before the war, had not expected the mine to play an important part. In a war on the surface of the sea the weaker navy would no doubt use such a weapon to hamper the movements of its superior antagonist: but for the stronger fleet, the fewer minefields the better. These conclusions, which at the time were not ill-founded, were upset by the changes for which the prolongation of the war gave time. At the outset the British mines were few and inefficient. It was even stated in a German Order that 'British mines generally do not explode.' This was an exaggeration: but we were certainly at fault in the matter.

At the end of April, 1916, an attempt was made by the

Dover Force, under Admiral Sir Reginald Bacon, to blockade the Flanders U-boats by a long and extensive barrage off the Belgian coast. This was completed by May 7. It consisted of 18 miles of moored mines and nets guarded from May to October by day patrols. U.B. 13 was destroyed by one of its mines the day after the barrage was laid, and an immediate diminution of U-boat activity in the North Sea and the Channel followed. This was not unnaturally attributed to the new barrage and gave the Dover Command an exaggerated idea of its value. We now know that it was to Admiral Scheer's impulsive recall of the High Sea Fleet U-boat flotillas, and not to the Dover barrage that the marked improvement of these months was due, for only one U-boat was destroyed by its mines; nor did it seriously impede their movements in and out.

Efforts to improve the quality of the British mines had been unceasing since the beginning of the war. It was not until the autumn of 1917 that the new 'horned' mines became available in large quantities. The improvement of the new type upon the old cannot be better measured than by the fact that out of forty-one U-boats destroyed by mines only five were prior to September, 1917. No less than 15,700 mines were laid in the Heligoland Bight during 1917 and 21,000 more in 1918, mainly by the 20th Destroyer Flotilla working from the Humber. This attempt to block in the U-boats developed into a protracted struggle between British mine-layers and German mine-sweepers. The enemy was forced to escort the U-boats both on their inward and outward journey with a whole array of mine-sweepers, of specially constructed ships with concrete-filled bows called 'barrier-breakers,' and torpedo boats. These escorts had to be protected, and from 1917 onwards the main occupation of the High Sea Fleet was the support of its sweeping forces working far afield on the submarine routes. As time went on the difficulties of egress and ingress increased. The 'ways' or swept channels in the Bight were frequently closed, and in October, 1917, homeward-bound submarines

began to be sent round by the Kattegat. Early in 1918 about
1,400 deep mines were laid in the Kattegat but could not be
patrolled. The intensive mining of the Bight failed to achieve
success because of the difficulties of attacking the German
sweeping craft and the lack of destroyers for the patrol of the
Kattegat. The effort however destroyed several U-boats,
and increased their time on passage to and from the trade
routes.

During 1917 the failure of the 1916 Barrage across the Dover
Straits had been total. From February to November U-boats
continued to pass through it at the rate of about twenty-four
a month. The Dover passage saved a small Flanders U-boat
nearly eight days on its fourteen-days' cruise, and a larger
boat from the Bight six days out of twenty-five. It was
decided to make a fresh attempt with all the improved ap-
pliances now at hand. On November 21 a new deep minefield
was laid between the Varne and Gris Nez. When no fewer
than twenty-one U-boats passed through this in the first
fortnight, a sharp controversy arose at the Admiralty. Some
authorities supported the contentions of the Dover Command
that the barrage was largely successful and that additional
patrolling was impracticable. Others held that an intensive
patrol and the use of search-lights and flares at night to make
the U-boats dive into the mines would achieve great results.
About this time, and partly in connection with this discussion,
Sir John Jellicoe was replaced as First Sea Lord by Admiral
Wemyss, and Admiral Bacon was succeeded in the Dover
Command by Admiral Keyes. Keyes revolutionised the
situation. He redoubled the patrols, and by night the barrage
from end to end became as bright as Piccadilly. The German
destroyers from Ostend and Zeebrugge attempted to break
down the patrols by sudden raids. They were repulsed in
fierce night actions and the watch maintained with ever-
increasing efficiency. Nine U-boats perished in the Dover
area between January and May, 1918, and four more by

September. As early as February the Bight boats ceased to use the Straits, and by April the Flanders boats had largely abandoned it. In September only two boats passed through, one of which was destroyed on its return.

The famous story of the blocking of Zeebrugge on St. George's Day by Admiral Keyes and the Dover Force cannot be repeated here. It may well rank as the finest feat of arms in the Great War, and certainly as an episode unsurpassed in the history of the Royal Navy. The harbour was completely blocked for about three weeks and was dangerous to U-boats for a period of two months. Although the Germans by strenuous efforts partially cleared the entrance after some weeks for U-boats, no operations of any importance were ever again carried out by the Flanders destroyers. The results of Admiral Keyes' command at Dover reduced the Allied losses in the English Channel from about twenty to six a month, and the minefields laid by the Flanders boats fell from thirty-three a month in 1917 to six a month in 1918. These results, which constitute a recognisable part of the general victory, were achieved notwithstanding the fact that the numbers of U-boats in commission were maintained by new building at about two hundred.

The attempts to mine in the Heligoland Bight had been frustrated by the German sweeping operations, closely supported by the High Sea Fleet. It was thought that a more distant barrage, under the direct watch and ward of the Grand Fleet, might succeed. In 1918 an ambitious scheme for establishing a line of guarded minefields across the 180 miles of water between Norway and the Orkney Islands was developed by the British and American navies. Enormous quantities of materials, regardless of cost or diversion of effort, were employed upon this supreme manifestation of defensive warfare. The large centre section was laid entirely by Americans, the Orkney section by the British, and the Norway section by the two navies in combination. The Americans used a special type of mine with antennæ that exploded the charge on coming into contact with the metal hull. They laid no less than 57,000 mines, a large number of which exploded prematurely shortly after being laid. The British contribution was about 13,000 mines, but some of these were not laid deep enough for surface craft to pass over and had in consequence to be swept up. The efficiency of this enormous material effort cannot be judged, for the minefield was barely completed when the Armistice was signed. It is known however that two U-boats were damaged on the centre section, and four may possibly have been destroyed on the Orkney section.

The ever-increasing efficiency of the Anti-Submarine Organisation during 1918 also mastered the mine-laying tactics of the U-boats. Closer co-operation between the British Intelligence and Mine Sweeping Divisions, the rapid distribution of news, the firmer control of shipping and the use of the 'Otter'[1] all played their part. One hundred and twenty-three British merchant ships had been sunk by German mines in 1917. In 1918 this number was reduced to 10. All other anti-submarine devices were developed with ceaseless ingenuity. Aircraft, hydrophones and special types of mines levied an increasing toll upon the U-boats. During 1918 high hopes were based on systematic hunting tactics, and trawler flotillas equipped with ingenious listening devices were assembled in the northern area for this purpose. Several contacts were made, but the U-boats escaped by going dead slow so that their movements could not be detected by the instruments; and we could not provide enough destroyers over such wide areas to exhaust their accumulators.

The final phase of the U-boat war saw the rôles of the combatants reversed. It was the U-boat and not the merchant ship that was hunted. The experiences of U.B.110 on her first cruise may serve as an example. She sailed from Zee-

[1] A species of submerged wire cutter towed on both bows for cutting the mooring ropes of mines.

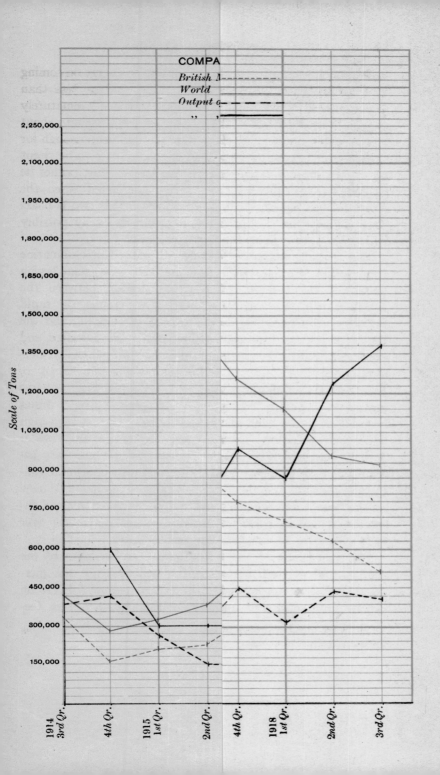

COMPA

British N ----------
World
Output – – – –
„ „ ━━━━

Scale of Tons

2,250,000
2,100,000
1,950,000
1,800,000
1,650,000
1,500,000
1,350,000
1,200,000
1,050,000
900,000
750,000
600,000
450,000
300,000
150,000

1914 3rd Qr.
4th Qr.
1915 1st Qr.
2nd Qr.
4th Qr.
1918 1st Qr.
2nd Qr.
3rd Qr.

brugge on July 5, 1918. Even before she had joined the
Flanders Flotilla she had been attacked by two aeroplanes.
Every day from July 7 onwards her log records the dropping
of depth charges around her in ever-increasing numbers until
the 18th, when twenty-six exploded close at hand. She was
only able to fire two torpedoes during the cruise. The first
one damaged an oil ship, but she could not see the result of
the second owing to an immediate and violent counter-attack
by destroyers. On the 19th, when attempting to attack a
convoy, her diving rudders were damaged by a depth charge
dropped from a motor launch; and while endeavouring to
submerge she was rammed and sunk by a destroyer. In these
latter days a Flanders U-boat could hope for only six voyages
before meeting its dark doom. The unceasing presentiment of
a sudden and frightful death beyond human sight or succour,
the shuddering concussions of the depth charges, the continual
attacks of escort vessels, the fear of annihilation at any moment
from mines, the repeated hair-breadth escapes, produced a
state of nervous tension in the U-boat crews. Their original
high morale declined rapidly during 1918 under an intolerable
strain. The surrender of more than one undamaged submarine
and numerous cases of boats putting back for small repairs a
few days after leaving harbour showed that even in this valiant
age the limits of human endurance had been reached.

The various stages of the U-boat war and its strange conditions have now been examined. No sooner had the German
war leaders taken their irrevocable decision to begin the
unlimited attack on commerce than the Russian Revolution,
by rendering their situation less desperate, removed the
principal impulsion. No sooner had the unlimited U-boat
warfare forced the United States into the field against Germany
than the effectiveness of the U-boats began to decline. The
month that saw President Wilson jingling among his Cavalrymen to the Senate to cast the life energy of a nation of a
hundred and twenty millions into the adverse scales marked

also the zenith of the U-boat attack. Never again did Germany equal the April sinkings. Many months of grievous losses and haunting anxiety lay before the Islanders and their Allies, and immense diversions—some needless—of straitened resources hampered their military effort. But with every month the sense of increasing mastery grew stronger. At one time the plotted curves of sinkings and replacements which our graphs revealed seemed a veritable 'writing on the wall.' But the awful characters faded steadily. The autumn of 1917, which was to have seen the fulfilment of German dreams, came, passed, and left us safer. By the end of the year it was certain we should not succumb. It was certain moreover that the war could be carried on until the power of the United States could if necessary be fully exerted on the battlefields of Europe. By the middle of 1918 the submarine campaign had been definitely defeated; and though new U-boats replaced those destroyed, every month added to their perils, to the restriction of their depredations and to the demoralization of their crews. The weapon purchased so dearly by the German war leaders had first been blunted and then broken in their hands. It remained for them only to pay the price, and meet the fury of the world in arms. But from this they did not shrink.

CHAPTER XVI

THE GERMAN CONCENTRATION IN THE WEST

The Man-Power Crisis—The Gathering Storm—Cabinet and G.H.Q.
—My Memorandum of December 8—Man-Power and Strategy—
Proposals for Increasing the Supply—Further Resources—General
Summary of British Resources—My Speech at Bedford—The
Policy of the War Cabinet—Extension of the British Front—The
General Allied Reserve—The Versailles Committee—Sir William
Robertson Dismissed—A Visit to the Canadians—The New De-
fensive Tactics—Sir Henry Wilson—His Qualities and Services—
A Favourable Atmosphere—My Survey of March 5—How to Obtain
a Decision—Means of Continuous Forward Progression—The Four
New Arms—A Different Distribution—Mechanical Developments—
The Mechanical Battle—The Reduced Scale and Intensity of the
War—The Agonizing Deadlock—The 300 Kilometre Battle.

AN acute crisis in Man-Power followed the prodigal
campaign of 1917, and a prolonged and searching examination of our remaining resources was made by the War
Cabinet. The British Infantry, on whom the brunt of the
slaughter had fallen, were woefully depleted. The battalions
were far below their proper strength, and even so, largely
composed of new drafts. The losses of the artillery both in
men and guns destroyed were also most severe. The loss in
officers was out of all proportion even to the great losses of
the rank and file. The task had throughout demanded an
unprecedented degree of sacrifice from regimental officers.
More than five thousand had been killed outright and over
fifteen thousand had been wounded in the Paschendale
offensive. This loss was especially difficult to replace; could
never in fact be fully replaced. We had every reason to expect
that the main fighting of 1918 in France would fall upon Great
Britain. The French, who had begun with the unequalled
slaughter of 1914 and had ever since been engaged on a scale

of nearly one hundred and twenty divisions, must necessarily and naturally be expected to reserve their remaining strength—grand it proved to be—for supreme emergencies. It was now certain that the United States, in spite of their utmost efforts and passionate desire to share the suffering, could not play more than a minor part in the actual battles. Only eight or nine American divisions were in fact due to enter the line before the summer was far spent. Substantial help had been sent perforce from the Western Front to Italy, and none could be expected in return. We had also almost the whole burden of the war against Turkey on our hands; and Allenby, so far from being able to release divisions, was continually pressing, not only for drafts but for reinforcements. Additional forces, both British and Indian, were required for the army in Mesopotamia; and finally the Salonica Front, on which we bore our share, was a constant drain. It was in these grave circumstances that we had to anticipate a German onslaught far exceeding in power and fury anything that had yet been experienced.

The final collapse of Russia had liberated enormous masses of German and Austrian troops. During the whole of the winter the movement of divisions and guns from the Eastern to the Western Front, and to a lesser extent against Italy, was unceasing. How great this movement actually was we could not measure exactly, but the Intelligence reports, with which I endeavoured to saturate myself, revealed week after week an unending flow of men and material to the West. Surveying the forces on both sides in the main theatre, it could not be doubted that by the spring Germany would have for the first time in the war, not even excepting the original invasion, a large numerical preponderance on the Western Front. Moreover, the divisions coming from Russia would, by the opening of the new campaign, have had nearly a year without serious fighting in which to recuperate and train. All our fighting units, on the other hand, had been decimated fivefold in the

last six months of 1917. Finally, in addition to the masses
of German and Austrian artillery released from the Russian
Front, the enemy had captured at least four thousand guns
from Russia and two thousand from Italy, together with immense supplies of war material of all kinds.

Sir Douglas Haig vehemently and naturally called for all
the officers and men required to bring his divisions up to full
strength at the earliest possible moment. Robertson supported him, and was evidently seriously alarmed. From my
central position between the Army and the War Cabinet, with,
I believe, the whole information available in my possession and
with constant intimate access to the Prime Minister, I never
ceased to press for the immediate reinforcement of Sir Douglas
Haig. Mr. Lloyd George viewed with horror the task imposed
on him of driving to the shambles by stern laws the remaining
manhood of the nation. Lads of eighteen and nineteen, elderly
men up to forty-five, the last surviving brother, the only son
of his mother (and she a widow), the father the sole support of
the family, the weak, the consumptive, the thrice wounded—
all must now prepare themselves for the scythe. To meet the
German onslaught when it came—if it came—everything
must be thrown in: but the Prime Minister feared lest our last
resources should be expended in another Paschendale.

It was in December that the shadow fell darkly upon the
military mind. Up till then the Cabinet had been assured
that all was going well in the West, and that—granted the
drafts—the New Year could be faced with confidence. At
the Ministry of Munitions we had long been instructed to
prepare for a renewed thirty weeks' offensive beginning in the
earliest spring. With the end of Paschendale came the end
of illusions. A sudden sinister impression was sustained by
the General Staff. The cry for a fresh offensive died away.
The mood swung round to pure defence—and against heavy
odds. It was a revolution at once silent and complete. I
responded to it with instant relief. The War Cabinet how-

ever continued for some time to rest themselves upon the confident declarations of the Generals made in September in advocacy of perseverance at Paschendale. They did not readily conform to the military *volte-face* and were sceptical of tales so utterly at variance with those of a few weeks before.

I urged that the Cabinet should send all the men that were needed to reconstitute the Army, and should at the same time forbid absolutely any resumption of the offensive. The Prime Minister however did not feel that, if the troops were once in France, he would be strong enough to resist those military pressures for an offensive which had so often overborne the wiser judgment of Statesmen. He therefore held, with all his potent influence, to a different policy. He sanctioned only a moderate reinforcement of the Army, while at the same time gathering in England the largest possible numbers of reserves. In this way he believed he would be able alike to prevent a British offensive and to feed the armies during the whole course of the fearful year which was approaching. This was in fact achieved. But I held, and hold still, that the War Cabinet should have been resolute, as I believe it would have been found strong enough, at once to support and to restrain the High Command in France. I set forth in the following secret Memorandum my views in detail.

Man-Power and the Situation

To the War Cabinet.

December 8, 1917.

1. IT is not possible to settle the question of man-power without a clear idea of the plan of campaign. The Ministry of National Service is naturally bound to tabulate the demands of the various Departments, set their existing resources against them, and show the resulting deficit. But these demands are a mere aggregate of separate and independent departmental requirements and not, as they should be, the expression of a general scheme of war. If a plan of campaign suited to the actual facts of next year, as far as we can foresee them, were

made out, it seems certain to me that the total demand could be substantially reduced.

2. For instance, the calculations of military requirements have been based upon a continuance of the kind of offensive action which we have pursued during the last two years, whereas the balance of forces next year will clearly not permit a continuance of that policy on the same scale nor to the same degree. It is vital to us to have in the field at the opening of the Spring campaign a British army stronger and better equipped than we have ever had before, because the burden thrown upon it is going to be greater than before. On the other hand, this army, once raised and restored to its full efficiency and strength, must be husbanded and not consumed. It must be an army crouched and not sprawled; an army with a large proportion of divisions in reserve at full strength, resting and training; an army sustained by every form of mechanical equipment, including, especially, tanks and aeroplanes, and possessing the greatest possible lateral mobility. What is required therefore is an immediate large draft of men to raise the Army to its fullest strength and to give it the greatest possible springing power and striking power. At the same time this power, when gained, must be scrupulously and jealously guarded and even hoarded, and not reduced or impaired except to meet vital emergencies.

These two aspects must be kept simultaneously in mind—

(a) An immediate raising of the Army to the highest possible strength; and
(b) Its jealous conservation when raised.

Our rôle and only chance of escaping defeat is to bridge the long intervening months before the Americans can become a decisive factor; and as we cannot tell what emergencies we may have to meet in the meanwhile, we must not only mobilise our greatest possible strength, but keep it in hand to guard against unforeseeable contingencies.

3. To say that we should raise our army to the highest possible offensive power by no means implies that it should be immediately launched upon a general offensive. To say, on the other hand, that the general rôle of the British armies will be 'an active defensive' by no means precludes the striking of sudden heavy blows on our own initiative, nor the

power of vehement counter-attack. There is therefore great scope for generalship in a campaign of this character, and a possibility of a certain number of brilliant military episodes of first-rate importance. The dominant principle however, from which there must be no swerving, is that we shall be a holding force, endeavouring to maintain, with the least possible loss, a situation which cannot be improved decisively except by the arrival of a great American army. . . .

5. A Commander-in-Chief in the field is entitled to know from his Government—

(a) What his general rôle is to be.
(b) What are to be his monthly incomes of men and shell tonnage.
(c) What condition the Army is to be left in at the end of the campaign in point of numbers and efficiency.

Within these limits, his discretion should be unfettered.

6. The Ministry of National Service assumes that the demand of the Navy for 90,000 additional men should have priority above army needs, and he makes apparently no provision for combing or dilution, either in the Navy or in its civil establishments. Again, it is to be observed that the naval demands for men cannot be considered except in reference to the general plan of war. If the Navy had plans for offensive or amphibious action which might be expected to cause the enemy to withdraw large numbers of men from the existing battle fronts, justification for a substantial increase in the man-power at their disposal would be provided. But if, as may well be, it is considered that there are no prudent and practicable means of using the Navy in this manner, then it is difficult to see what good reasons there can be to increase the number of men at the disposal of the Admiralty. We are far stronger in proportion to the German fleet than we were at the beginning of the war, when they did not venture to attack us. We are probably employing, apart from shipbuilding, three or four times as many men for naval purposes as they are, and in addition to this, besides the navies of the European Allies, there is the American fleet—the third strongest in the world.

There are many more detailed aspects of the use of naval personnel which demand instructed and critical examination. In a crisis like this every man counts, and no department or branch of our fighting forces has a right to special privileges.

The construction of warships other than for anti-submarine warfare also makes a heavy demand on labour and valuable materials.

7. There are at present employed on shipbuilding and munitions work over 3,000,000 men and women. A plan can be submitted for providing from this total 100,000 category A. men for the Army. The plan would include the 'clean cut' for category A. men below the age of 24, who are estimated at about 55,000, in munitions and shipbuilding. The loss on shipbuilding and marine engineering would have to be made good by transferring older men from other munitions work. This would be practicable. . . .

9. The next great resource of man-power which should now be drawn upon is the Army at home. This at present comprises upwards of 1,400,000 men who are explained or excused in various ways. In order that this resource shall be rendered effective for the armies on the Western front, we must face the institution of defensive battalions for holding quiet and non-significant sectors of the line. The actual military arrangements obviously require careful but not necessarily prolonged study. 150 battalions of 1,000 men each should certainly be obtained from this source and woven into our scheme for maintaining the Western front and the efficiency of our armies next year.

10. I have already drawn attention to the extraordinary increase in the standards of home defence against invasion which has taken place since the early periods of the war. The continental military crisis now is as intense as it was in the days of the Marne and the Yser. There is no reason to assume that invasion is less impossible now than it was then. There are in fact a wealth of reasons to the contrary which could easily be stated if desired. It is a fair proposition that, apart from any men taken in the shape of garrison battalions from the troops at home not included in the home defence forces, there should also be at least 50,000 men taken, say, in brigades from the existing home defence forces, and used for holding quiet sectors of the front in France.

The garrison of Ireland requires to be reconsidered from the point of view of the actual work it might have to do; that is to say, not the conduct of military operations in the ordinary sense but the suppression of sporadic disorders and local rebellions. Armoured motor-cars, machine-gun cyclists, the older pattern of aeroplanes, and a few tanks for street fighting seem to be features which require special development. It is for consideration whether 10,000 serviceable men could not be found from this source for service in ordinary or in garrison battalions abroad.

The total available from the military forces in Great Britain and Ireland should not be estimated at less than 210,000 men.

11. Mechanical engines afford an important means of multiplying man-power. The tanks have proved themselves in appropriate circumstances not only to be a substitute for bombardment but an indispensable adjunct to infantry. In the attack in Flanders we gained 54 square miles with an expenditure of 465,000 tons of ammunition costing 84,000,-000l., and probably over 300,000 casualties. The offensive at Cambrai, depending as it did entirely upon the surprise use of tanks on a large scale, gained 42 square miles with an expenditure of 36,000 tons of shell, costing 6,600,000l., and with a loss of life which, had the operation been confined to its early and fruitful stage, would have not exceeded 10,000 casualties.[1]

There is much to be said in modification of crude figures and comparisons of this kind. But when everything has been said the conclusion presented is overwhelming.

Powerful as the tanks have proved themselves in surprise offensives on suitable ground, they are still more valuable in counter-attack. In this case they would be moving over ground with which they were familiar, and against an enemy necessarily unprepared with any special arrangements to receive them. They are immune from panic, and in their advance must carry forward with them the infantry counter-attack. It would be lamentable if, for want of men at this stage of the war, and with its lessons so cruelly written, we should not be allowed to develop these weapons to our highest manufacturing capacity. Are we really to keep in being, at a time when every man is precious, when every ton of stores counts, 30,000 or 40,000 cavalry with their horses, when these admirable cavalrymen would supply the personnel for the greatest development of mechanical warfare both for offence

[1] It was actually much less.

and defence in tanks, in armoured cars, and on motor-cycles that has ever yet been conceived? . . .

12. To sum up, the following proposals are put forward as a basis for examination. Sir Auckland Geddes' figures show that without recourse to fresh legislation there is a deficit on existing naval and military demands of approximately 645,000 men. It is suggested that this should be met as follows:—

(a) Reduction of monthly wastage through the adoption of an active defensive in the place of the continuous offensive of this year. Six months at 30,000 a month instead of 50,000 . . . . . . = 120,000
(b) The Navy 'living on its own' and through American resources. Reduced demand . . . . = 90,000
(c) Munitions and shipbuilding (no diminution in total shipbuilding) . . . . = 100,000
(d) Garrison battalions of soldiers serving at home . = 150,000
(e) Garrison or sedentary brigades or divisions from home defence and Ireland . . . . . = 60,000
(f) Coal-mines, agriculture, railways, and balance of men as proposed by Sir Auckland Geddes . . . = 80,000

Total . . . . = 600,000

13. It is worth while considering other resources of manpower to which we should look, not merely as alternatives but as supplements and additions, viz.:—

(a) Raising the age to 50, as has long been done in Germany, Austria, and France (apart from larger numbers available for defensive units) 110,000
(b) Extending compulsion to Ireland 200,000
(c) American troops training, first in platoons, then in companies, and next in battalions, with the British army (200 battalions) 200,000
(d) Developments of mechanical warfare and lateral mobility multiply men but cannot be numerically appraised.

14. It is clear that with these extensive and varied resources at our disposal, we have the means of meeting the prime need of the situation, viz.: to meet the spring campaign with the British Army stronger in every respect than any we have previously put in the field; all its units full; a large propor-

tion of divisions resting and training, thus giving us a strategic reserve, in the Prime Minister's phrase 'an Army of Manœuvre'; an unprecedented development of mechanical and aeronautical warfare; and very large labour forces for defensive works, communications, and services behind the line. This can certainly be done if action is taken now in the same spirit as it would be undoubtedly taken and has in most cases been already taken by the enemy with whom we are fighting. Moreover it can be done without interfering in any serious degree with our war against the submarines, with our defence against invasion, or with our production of munitions.

Nearly all these specific measures, which were at this time contrary to the views of the War Cabinet, were taken or resolved on after the catastrophe of March 21. Taken in January, they would have prevented it.

I also made, under all proper guard, a speech at Bedford on December 11 in the same sense.

'Two months ago I stated in London that the war was entering upon its sternest phase, but I must admit that the situation at this moment is more serious than it was reasonable two months ago to expect. The country is in danger as it has not been since the battle of the Marne saved Paris, and the battles of Ypres and of the Yser saved the Channel ports. The cause of the Allies is now in danger. The future of the British Empire, and of democracy, and of civilisation hang, and will continue to hang for a considerable period, in a balance and an anxious suspense. It is impossible, even if it were desirable, to conceal these facts from our enemies. It would be folly not to face them boldly ourselves. . . .

'Anyone can see for himself what has happened in Russia. Russia has been thoroughly beaten by the Germans. Her great heart has been broken, not only by German might, but by German intrigue; not only by German steel, but by German gold. Russia has fallen on the ground prostrate in exhaustion and in agony. No one can tell what fearful vicissitudes will come to Russia, or how or when she will arise, but arise she will. It is this melancholy event which has prolonged the war, that has robbed the French, the British and the Italian armies of the prize that was perhaps almost within their reach this summer; it is this event, and this event alone, that has exposed us to perils and sorrows and sufferings which we have not deserved, which we cannot avoid, but under which we shall not bend.

'There never was a moment in this war when the practical steps which we ought to take showed themselves more plainly, or when the choice presented to us was so brutally clear as it is to-night, or when there was less excuse for patriotic men to make the mistake of being misled by sophistries and dangerous counsels. . . .

'What is the one great practical step we must take without a day's delay? We must raise the strength of our army to its highest point. A heavier strain will be thrown upon this army than it has ever had to bear before. We must see that it is stronger than it has ever been before. Do not put too heavy a burden on those heroic men by whose valiant efforts we exist from day to day. Husband their lives, conserve and accumulate their force. Every division of our army must be raised to full strength; every service—the most scientific, the most complex—must be thoroughly provided; we must make sure that in the months to come a large proportion of our army is resting, refreshing, and training behind the front line ready to spring like leopards upon the German hordes. Masses of guns, mountains of shells, clouds of aeroplanes—all must be ready, all must be there; we have only to act together, and we have only to act at once.'

These official or public arguments were reinforced by the strongest personal appeals. Nothing however had the slightest effect. The Prime Minister and his colleagues in the War Cabinet were adamant. Their policy was not decided without full deliberation. They were definitely opposed to any renewal of the British offensive in France. They wished the British and French armies to observe during 1918 a holding and defensive attitude. They wished to keep a tight control over their remaining man-power until the arrival of the American millions offered the prospect of decisive success. In the meanwhile action in Palestine, with forces almost inappreciable in the scale of the Western Front, might drive Turkey out of the war, and cheer the public mind during a long and grievous vigil. They were fully informed of the growing German concentration against Haig, and repeatedly discussed it. But they believed that the Germans if they attacked would encounter the same difficulties as had so long baffled us, and that our armies were amply strong enough for defence. Haig was accordingly left to face the spring with an army whose 56 infantry divisions were reduced from a thirteen to a ten-battalion basis,[1] and with three instead of five cavalry divisions,[2] which in the absence of alternative methods were at last to render valuable service.

But this was not the end of his trials. The French, also living in a world of illusions, now came forward with a vehement demand that the British should take over a larger part of the front. A cursory glance at the map shows that the French with 100 divisions comprising 700,000 rifles held 480 kilometres of front, whereas 56 British divisions comprising 504,000 rifles only held 200 kilometres. In other words, the British with more than two-thirds of the French rifle strength held less than one-third of the front. But this was a very superficial test. Large portions of the French front were in continual quiescence, and the weak railway communications opposite them excluded the possibility of a serious hostile offensive. The British, on the other hand, held nearly all the most active front, and had opposite to them, even in January, a larger proportion of German divisions than were marshalled against the French Army. Against the long French front were arrayed 79 German divisions, while no fewer than 69 stood before the short British sector. Moreover, the German concentration against the British front was growing week by week, and it was already extremely probable that the first and main thrust would be delivered upon them. Further, the French had not fought a heavy battle since April and May,

[1] Or from twelve to nine, if the Pioneer Battalion is excluded.
[2] Two Indian cavalry divisions were sent from France to Palestine.

1917, while the British Army had maintained an almost continuous offensive, suffering, as we have seen, calamitous losses. Finally, the French soldier enjoyed nearly three times as much leave to visit his home as his British comrade; that is to say, there were in proportion three times as many French rifles absent from the line at any given moment as there were British.

Under pressure both from the French and the British Governments, Haig had agreed in December to extend his front by fourteen miles as far south as Barisis; and this relief was effected in February. A further demand by the French that the British front should be extended to Berry-au-Bac thirty miles farther south-east, though backed with the threatened resignation of Monsieur Clémenceau, was successfully resisted under a similar threat by the British Commander-in-Chief.

The continued friction and want of confidence between Sir William Robertson and Mr. Lloyd George came to a head at the beginning of February. The Prime Minister was moving cautiously but tirelessly towards the conception of a unified command. He did not yet feel strong enough to disclose his purpose. A proposal which obviously involved placing the British armies under a French Commander was one which he judged as yet beyond his strength to carry. It was a hazardous issue on which to challenge the joint resignations both of Sir William Robertson and Sir Douglas Haig. It is probable that the War Cabinet would not have been united in its support; and that the Liberal opposition would have been unanimous against it. The Prime Minister had therefore so far suspended his wishes that speaking of an independent generalissimo he told the House of Commons in December: 'I am utterly opposed to that suggestion. It would not work. It would produce real friction, and might produce not merely friction between the armies, but friction between the nations and the Governments.'

Nevertheless, Mr. Lloyd George continued by a series of

extremely laborious and mystifying manœuvres to move steadily forward towards his solution. On January 30, at the meeting of the Supreme War Council at Versailles, he secured a decision to create a general reserve of thirty divisions and to entrust it to a Committee representing Britain, Italy, the United States and France, with General Foch at its head. This proposal constitutes his answer and that of the War Cabinet to the charge of imprudently lowering the strength of the British Army in France in the face of the growing German concentration. There is no doubt that had this plan been put immediately into execution, and had Foch been armed with thirty divisions specifically assigned to the support of whatever part of the front was attacked, larger resources would have been secured to Haig in his approaching hour of supreme need. Haig did not however welcome the proposal. He declared that he had no divisions to spare for the general reserve, and that there were not even enough for the various army fronts. In such circumstances the earmarking of particular British divisions for service elsewhere could have been little more than a formality. None could have been taken from him unless the attack fell elsewhere.

The decision, like many others of the Supreme War Council, remained a dead letter; and events moved forward without the British Army receiving either the reinforcements for which Haig had pleaded or the reserves which Lloyd George had laboured to supply.

Although the thirty divisions were lacking, the Executive Committee to control them at Versailles was created. Sir William Robertson claimed that he, as Chief of the Imperial General Staff, should alone represent Great Britain upon it. This raised an issue upon which the Prime Minister felt himself strong enough to engage. He declared it a matter of fundamental principle that the two posts could not be held by one man. It was his undoubted intention to arm the Cabinet with an alternative set of military advisers whose opinions could be used to curb and correct the Robertson-Haig view, and so prevent a repetition of offensives like Paschendale. No doubt he would also have used the new body to promote schemes of war outside the Western Front. The arrangement was indefensible in principle, but in the aftermath of Paschendale its objects were worthy. Into the complications of the dispute and its manœuvres it is not necessary to enter here. On February 11, Robertson, returning to London, which he had somewhat imprudently quitted for a few days, was confronted by the Secretary of State for War with a note signed on February 9 by the Prime Minister. This reduced the functions of the C.I.G.S. to the limits which had existed before the Kitchener breakdown, and it prescribed the independent functions of the British Military Representative on the Versailles Committee. Thirdly, it nominated Sir William Robertson Military Representative, and Sir Henry Wilson Chief of the Imperial General Staff. Robertson, astonished at his supersession, declined the appointment to Versailles on the ground that the arrangement was unsound. The post of C.I.G.S., although originally designed for Wilson, was then incontinently offered to Sir Herbert Plumer, who with equal promptitude refused it. Finally, it was offered again to Robertson on the reduced basis of the Prime Minister's Note. On February 16 Robertson recorded his refusal to agree to the conditions prescribed, and that same evening the Official Press Bureau announced that the Government had 'accepted his resignation.' He had in fact been dismissed. Lord Derby, who did his best to compose the differences, also proffered his resignation, which was not accepted.

The principles of military duty on which Sir Douglas Haig invariably proceeded prevented him, even at this time of tension with the Government, from adding his own resignation to the dismissal of the Chief of the Imperial General Staff. On questions which in his view involved the safety of the British armies under his command, Sir Douglas Haig—right or wrong—was, whenever necessary, ready to resign. But these constituted the sole exceptions which he allowed himself to make in his obedience. Had any motive of personal intrigue been present in his mind, the crisis between the High Command and the Civil Power would have been gravely aggravated. The position of the Government at this time was strong and the issue one on which they could rely on public support. The Prime Minister did not flinch. Nevertheless Haig's retention, without comment, of his post was received with relief by the anxious War Cabinet; and Sir Henry Wilson was speedily appointed to the vacant chair in Whitehall.

It would certainly not be just to assume in these transactions that any of the parties were influenced otherwise than by public duty. But beneath the bald record of events the clash is plain. Both the Prime Minister and Sir William Robertson were in deadly earnest, both measured forces, and both knew the risks they ran. It was impossible for the two men to work together any longer. The situation at the centre of power had become intolerable. Action was long overdue. It was a pity it could not have taken a simpler form.

Sir William Robertson was an outstanding military personality. His vision as a strategist was not profound, but his outlook was clear, well-drilled and practical. During his tenure he had reintroduced orderly methods of dealing with War Office problems, and had revivified the General Staff system. He had no ideas of his own, but a sensible judgment negative in bias. He represented professional formalism expressed in the plainest terms. He held a conception of war policy wholly opposed to the views set out in these volumes, but honestly and consistently maintained. I was glad, as Secretary of State for War, when after the victory he eventually retired from the Army, to submit a recommendation to the King which enabled his long and honourable career from the rank of a private soldier to end with the baton of a Field Marshal.

In the stresses of this internal disturbance I took no part. I was on the front during the whole week busily occupied, and it was only on my return that I learned the inner facts from various actors in the drama. The view which I took of my own work made it necessary for me to keep continually in touch with the actual conditions of the fighting line. The Commander-in-Chief accorded me the fullest liberty of movement in the British zone, and placed every facility at my disposal. I was most anxious to understand by personal observation the latest methods of holding the line which were involved in the preparations for a great defensive battle. I stayed with General Lipsett, commanding the 3rd Canadian Division, and under his deeply instructed guidance examined minutely from front to rear the whole of the sector which he occupied opposite to Lens.

Very different was the state of the line from what I had known it to be when serving with the guards in 1915 or as a Battalion Commander in 1916. The system of continuous trenches with their barbed-wire networks, their parapets, firing-steps, traverses and dugouts, the first line of which was manned in great strength and often constituted the strongest line of resistance, had vanished. Contact with the enemy was maintained only by a fringe of outposts, some of which were fortified, while others trusted merely to concealment. Behind these over a distance of two or three thousand yards were sited intricate systems of machine-gun nests, nearly all operating by flank fire and mutually supporting each other. Slender communication trenches enabled these to be approached and relieved by night. The barbed-wire networks, instead of being drawn laterally in a continuous belt across the front, lay obliquely with intervals so as to draw the attacker into avenues mercilessly swept by machine-gun fire. Open spaces between important points were reserved for the full fury of the protecting barrages. This was the Battle Zone. Two thousand yards or so farther in the rear were the field battery positions.

Strong works to which the long disused word 'redoubt' was applied, and deep grids of trenches and deeper dugouts elaborately camouflaged, provided for the assembling and maintenance of the supporting troops. Behind these again in modest and obscure recesses lay the Brigade Headquarters; behind which again the groups of heavy and medium batteries were disposed in studied irregular array. Favoured by beautiful weather and a quiet day, we were able by taking care to make our way into the ruins of Avion village, in which in twos and threes the keen-eyed Canadian sharpshooters maintained their ceaseless bickering against the German outposts fifty or a hundred yards away.

I must frankly admit that all that I saw, both in the line and of the minutely perfected organisation far to the rear, inspired me with confidence in the strength of the defensive system which had gradually developed as the war proceeded. Holding the convictions which this volume describes of the relative power of offence and defence under modern conditions, I looked forward, at least so far as this sector was concerned, to the day when the Germans would taste a measure of that bitter draught our armies had been made to drink so long. Alas the conditions here were by no means representative of the general state of the line.

*   *   *   *   *

It is no disparagement of the qualities of Sir William Robertson to record the very great pleasure with which I learned of the appointment of Sir Henry Wilson to be Chief of the Staff. We had known each other for many years. I had met him first by the banks of the Tugela in February, 1900, and my first picture of him is a haggard but jocular Major emerging from a bloody night's work in the Pieter's Hill fighting. It was in discussion with him from 1910 onwards that I had studied the problem of a war between France and Germany. Though I recorded at the time somewhat different conclusions about the opening phase from those on which he proceeded, my debt to him was very great. Never shall I forget the memorable forecast which in August, 1911, during the Agadir crisis, he had given to the Committee of Imperial Defence. At this period we were close confederates. The crisis passed away, and the Irish quarrel sundered our personal relations. A devoted son of Ulster, he resented with a passion which knew no bounds the Home Rule policy of the Liberal Government. During the intense days which preceded the British declaration of war upon Germany we were forced to meet on several occasions, but on a purely official basis. The mobilisation of the Fleet and the final decision to join France, in which I had played my part, carried all before them in Wilson's heart. But this I did not know, and it was with surprise that one August morning I received at the Admiralty a visit of ceremony from him on the eve of his departure for France. He had come to say that all past differences were obliterated and that we were friends again. He was opposed later on to the Dardanelles expedition. At that time he saw the War only in the light of the struggle in France. Had he commanded the central point of view, he would perhaps have had a different opinion. At any rate his policy as Chief of the Staff was far wider in its scope than the Western Front. But these disagreements did not, so far as I am aware, impair our personal relations; and when later on I served in France as a Battalion Commander, he showed me every courtesy and often discussed the whole situation, military and political, with the freedom we had practised at Whitehall in days when my position was superior. His appointment as Chief of the Staff led immediately to the closest harmony between the spheres of Strategy and Material. The conceptions of war which I held, and which these pages record, received from him a keen and pregnant welcome. Almost his first act was to raise the War Office demand for the Tank Corps from 18,000 to 46,000 men.

In Sir Henry Wilson the War Cabinet found for the first
time an expert adviser of superior intellect, who could explain
lucidly and forcefully the whole situation and give reasons for
the adoption or rejection of any course. Such gifts are, whether
rightly or wrongly, the object of habitual distrust in England.
But they are certainly a very great comfort in the transaction
of public business. Sir Henry Wilson constantly corrected the
clarity of his mind by whimsical mannerisms and modes of expression. He spoke in parables, used curious images and cryp-
tic phrases. He had a vocabulary of his own. The politicians
were 'frocks'; Clémenceau, always the 'Tiger.' He even addressed him as Tiger. His faithful Aide-de-Camp, Duncannon,
was 'the Lord.' He wantonly pronounced grotesquely the
names of French towns and Generals. In discussing the
gravest matters he used the modes of levity. 'Prime Minister,'
he began one day to the War Cabinet, at a meeting which I
attended, 'to-day I am Boche.' Then followed a penetrating
description of the situation from the standpoint of the German Headquarters. On another day he would be France or
Bulgaria, and always out of this affectation there emerged, to
my mind, the root of the matter in hand. But some ministers
were irritated. He did not go so far as Marshal Foch, who
sometimes gave a military description in pantomime; but their
methods of displaying a war proposition had much in common.

I can see him so clearly as I write, standing before the map
in the Cabinet Room giving one of his terse telegraphese ap-
preciations. 'This morning, Sir, a new battle.' (The reader
will recognise it when it comes.) 'This time it is we who have
attacked. We have attacked with two armies—one British,
one French. Sir Haig is in his train, Prime Minister, very uncomfortable, near the good city of Amiens. And Rawly[1] is in
his left hand and Debeny in his right. Rawly is using five
hundred tanks. It is a big battle, and we thought you would
not like us to tell you about it beforehand.' I cannot vouch for
the actual words, but this was the sense and manner of it.

[1] General Rawlinson.

We should be thankful that the future is veiled. I was to be present at another scene in this room. There was no Henry Wilson. The Prime Minister and I faced each other, and on the table between us lay the pistols which an hour before had drunk this loyal man's blood.

I have strayed alike from narrative and chronology to make in deep respect this reference to the most comprehending military mind of our day in Britain and to a soldier who, although he commanded no armies, exerted on occasion a profound and fortunate influence over the greatest events.

With Sir Henry Wilson, as his deputy, came the brilliant Harington, who at Plumer's side had won for the Second Army its unequalled reputation. I think I may say that in all that concerned the making of the weapons for a campaign in 1919, with their inevitable profound reactions upon its plans, we thought as one. He supported me in all my principal projects for the supply of the armies, and used, under Sir Henry Wilson, the whole power of the General Staff to carry forward the plans for the great mechanical battle which we trusted, however late in the day, would bring finality.

I had also in the War Office at this time a friend in General Furse, the Master-General of the Ordnance. He had commanded the Division in which I had served during the few months I was at the front, and we had many times argued out the kind of projects I was now in a position to put forward. To ensure the closest contact in the vast Artillery sphere I appointed him with Lord Milner's approval [1] to be an actual member of the Munitions Council. Thus all these far-reaching and, though subordinate, yet vital controls pulled together from this time forward, and we had to worry only about the enemy.

In this favourable atmosphere at the beginning of March I completed a general survey of the War ostensibly from the Munitions standpoint, and unfolded the argument for the mechanical battle.

[1] Lord Milner had now succeeded Lord Derby at the War Office.

To the War Cabinet.

March 5, 1918.

MUNITIONS PROGRAMME, 1919

1. So far as munitions are concerned, the year 1918 is settled for good or for ill. No decisive changes in our modes of warfare can be produced in time to influence the campaign now opening. But it is imperative to decide quite soon what the character of the campaign of 1919 is to be. It is no use considering such a question in October or November. Practically a whole year's notice is required for any great development in material. We ought to have made up our minds by the beginning of April what the main principles and general outlines of our munitions programme for 1919 are to be. I would ask that this task may be undertaken at once.

2. We are immediately confronted with the fundamental question 'How are we going to win the War in 1919?' It seems to me a reasonable expectation, if every effort is made and unity prevails, that by the end of this year we shall have established three very substantial facts which are now disputed: (i) either the German will have attacked in the West and have been repulsed, or he will have exposed himself incapable of delivering an offensive on a great scale; (ii) the submarine warfare will have entered upon a phase in which our tonnage will be greater at the end of every month, and not less as at present; (iii) the growing American Army will be becoming a real and great military factor. It is possible we may add a (iv) to this, viz., a definite and unmistakable ascendancy in the air both as regards numbers and quality. All these aims have of course to be fought for and worked for during the ensuing months. They are reasonable objects of endeavour. Failure to attain any of them would be disastrous to us. Our success, on the other hand, in attaining all of them will not necessarily be fatal to the enemy.

3. (*a*) We must further assume that a new front will be made against the enemy in the East by Japanese armies being brought as deeply as possible into Russia, and by every conceivable inducement being offered to Japan to come directly into collision and contact with the German forces. It will further be necessary to stop the spread of German influence towards India through Persia. This can only be done

by sending without delay sufficient troops to dominate the Persian situation, as was done by the Grand Duke in 1915 with such successful results. (*b*) We must assume that while Germany is absorbing and dragooning Russia Great Britain will continue to break up and devour Turkey as an offset, albeit unequal. (*c*) We may balance the chances of an internal collapse in Italy against those of an internal collapse in Austria, it being assumed however that we shall do as much to help Italy as Germany has done since the beginning of the war for her allies.

4. All these perilous matters being accomplished will bring us to the campaign of 1919, and if we get so far the question repeats itself, 'How are we going to win then?' If there is no method of winning then which military men can discover, it will certainly be argued by many that it would be better to make peace at the least unfavourable moment in the present year, abandoning altogether the hope of a decisive victory in the war. It therefore becomes of the very highest consequence to discover what is the best plan for 1919, and whether there is any plan or use we can make of our resources which will give us a reasonable hope of a military victory.

5. It is clear that a military victory (apart from internal collapse) can only be reached by offensive action, and that offensive action can only be based on overwhelming superiority in one form or another. Even if all the favourable assumptions made in the earlier paragraphs of this paper are borne out, it is clear that no overwhelming superiority will be available for us in several of the main elements of war. For instance, we cannot expect any sufficient preponderance in man-power in 1919, even with the American armies, to enable us to overwhelm by numbers the German front in the West. The best it is reasonable to hope is that the two sides will be of about the same relative strength as in 1917 before the Russian collapse. Even this is highly disputable. On the other hand we may fairly reckon on a good superiority in quality, which, added to the improvement in numbers, will give us once again in the West undoubtedly the stronger armies. Still, the margin will not be enough to offer any prospect of a military victory by man-power.

6. There does not either seem to be any good prospect of winning a military victory through an overwhelming superi-

ority in guns and shells. We are already at the limit of our
shell production. We cannot expect that the tonnage of 1919
will at the very best do more than enable us, having regard
to our depleting stocks, to maintain our 1918 standards.
These give us no marked superiority over the enemy. Further,
the limits of what can be effected by gun power have been
coming very clearly into view. We see that after a certain
point it tends to defeat its own purposes as an offensive
weapon, for the ground is so ploughed up by the necessary
artillery preparation that it is impossible for troops to advance
over it. It is a very practical and pregnant question at the
moment whether artillery has not been overdone, and whether
in the disposition of our resources for 1919 both personnel and
material should not be liberated from artillery for other forms
of warfare. I will return to this later.

7. Again, it is clear that our policy of blockade on which
the Navy have hitherto relied can no longer be counted upon
to produce decisive results now that the Germans have got
enormous portions of Russia at their disposal. Indeed we are
likely during the period under survey to suffer nearly as
much inconvenience and political instability through lack of
supplies as are our enemies.

I therefore return to the fundamental question. If you
cannot starve out your enemy, if you cannot bear him down
by numbers or blast him from your path with artillery, how
are you going to win?

8. I wish to avow however at this stage in the argument a
firm conviction that the method and the means do exist by
which in 1919 the German armies in the West could be decisively defeated and their front effectively broken up. No
proposition of this kind can be stated in terms of certainty,
because there are no certainties in war; but I believe that if
the right decisions are taken now, it should be possible to impart to the British armies in particular, and to the Allied
armies in general, *a means of continuous forward progression*
in 1919 which if successful would yield decisive results, and
that the chances of success are good enough to justify the
prolongation of the struggle in the meanwhile. I will proceed
to indicate in general terms the lines of thought to which attention should be directed in order to realise the result.

II

9. Wars have hitherto been conducted by infantry, cavalry and artillery, and these are the three recognised arms of the service. It has also been observed with some truth that 'the infantry is the Army, and uses the other arms as its adjuncts.' Whichever way the question is viewed, it is clear that there are no means of obtaining an overwhelming superiority sufficient to enable a continuous advance to be made by any developments which it is in our power to make in the infantry, cavalry, and artillery in 1919. However, in the present war at least four new arms of the highest consequence have come into being, viz.:—

> Aeroplanes,
> Tanks,
> Gas, and
> Machine guns.

If we are to obtain the necessary superiority and the means of effective progression against the enemy, it can only be by developments of a far-reaching character in these new methods of warfare.

10. And let it here be observed that every one of these four new arms has already played or shown itself capable of playing a decisive part in the present war, in spite of the fact that they have only been tardily and partially and doubtingly developed. For instance, it is the machine gun which has made the defensive hitherto invincible. Again, if either side possessed the power to drop not five tons but five hundred tons of bombs each night on the cities and manufacturing establishments of its opponent, the result would be decisive. If the Germans had used poison gas on a sufficiently large scale the first time they used it at all and before we were provided with effective masks, they could undoubtedly have broken up our whole front in the West. Similarly, if we had developed tanks in secret or at any rate in mystery till we had about 2,000, and then had used them as they were used at the battle of Cambrai, only on a much larger scale and with carefully husbanded reserves of infantry to follow them up, we in turn might have broken up the German front and driven their armies into a continuous retreat. We are clearly in the presence of new factors, all of which possess decisive qualities.

11. It must however be remembered that the total quantity of our resources is limited, and that the decision which has to be taken is one which involves the development of these new arms, both in men and material, to a very large extent at the expense of the old. Still, it is contended that this should be boldly faced, that we should create in order to attack the enemy in 1919 an army essentially different in its composition and methods of warfare from any that have yet been employed on either side. This would only be in accordance with the obvious principle that if you cannot get a sufficient superiority over your opponent in the same methods as he employs, you should break away and develop different and unexpected variants. Thus we may contemplate (a) relieving the want of man-power in the infantry, especially on defensive sectors of the front, by great increases of machine guns, automatic rifles, and the like; or (b) putting most of the cavalry into tanks or other mechanical vehicles; or (c) drawing upon the artillery and the material which supplies it, as far as may be needed, to raise chemical warfare to its proper proportionate position in our organisation. It is unnecessary to speak of the air, for that is already accepted. We have undoubtedly the power at the present time of making such decisions fully effective for 1919 if we act without delay and upon a carefully thought out and ruthlessly pursued plan. The question is essentially one of proportion, but it is not capable of being solved unless the old proportions are definitely put aside and revolutionary changes in the composition of the armies and in their methods of warfare are unhesitatingly faced.

12. On the other hand, we need not exaggerate the extent of the changes which would be necessary. Let us assume—the figures are of course only tokens—that at the present time our military effort in men and material combined is expressed as follows:—

Infantry, 40 per cent.
Artillery, 40 per cent.
Air, 10 per cent.
Cavalry, 3½ per cent.
Machine guns, 4 per cent.
Tanks, 2 per cent.
Gas, ½ per cent.

The kind of change that is suggested might be expressed as follows:—

Infantry, 35 per cent.
Artillery, 30 per cent.
Air, 15 per cent.
Cavalry, ½ per cent.
Machine guns, 7 per cent.
Tanks, 8 per cent.
Gas, 4½ per cent.

This would give us an army substantially different in its composition from that of its opponents, and capable of confronting him with offensive propositions fundamentally different in character from those which he has hitherto disposed of.

As stated above, the Air expansion is already practically conceded. The development of machine guns and automatic rifles is also to a great extent assured; but the two most vital of the new arms, namely tanks and gas, are at present only used on a miniature and experimental scale.

13. Yet in both of these we have immense advantages, inherent or acquired, over the enemy. Incomparably the most effective method of discharging gas is by liberating it from cylinders to form a gas cloud when the wind is favourable. In no other way can results on the largest scale be achieved. Although for some time we and the Germans have relied instead upon firing gas shells from guns or mortars, there is no doubt that the original method in spite of its difficulty and danger is by far the most formidable. It is undoubtedly possible if the wind is favourable to discharge gas over a wide front which, if the discharge is sufficiently prolonged or intense, will render all existing masks ineffectual. The supreme fact is that the wind is at least six times, and some say nine times, as favourable to us as it is to the enemy. We are mad not to avail ourselves of this overwhelming advantage. But with our present pitifully small gas service of perhaps 6,000 or 7,000 men we are only trifling with the problem.

14. Again, take tanks. Here our advantage is due to our having started far in advance of the enemy and having with painful slowness but extreme thoroughness explored the difficulties, tactical and manufacturing, of this highly complicated

arm. The element of novelty has now been thrown away, but numbers, quality, organisation, and training still afford us opportunities of the first order if we only had the wisdom and resolution to profit by them. The year 1919 is still at our disposal. It is undoubtedly within our power to construct in very large numbers armoured vehicles of various types, some to fight, some to pursue, some to cut wire and trample trenches, some to carry forward men or machine-gun parties, or artillery, or supplies, to such an extent and on such a scale that 150,000 to 200,000 fighting men can be carried forward certainly and irresistibly on a broad front and to a depth of 8 or 10 miles in the course of a single day. The resources are available, the knowledge is available, the time is available, the result is certain: nothing is lacking except the will. We have never been able to get out of the rut of traditional and conventional methods. We have never been able to plan on a sufficiently large scale, long in advance, and with the necessary force and authority to drive the policy through. We have instead only carried out a series of costly experiments, each of which has shown us the chance we have lost and exposed our thought to the enemy.

15. It surely lies with those who shake their heads to say on what alternative method of attack or on what alternative form of superiority they can rely to win a military victory in 1919. Where are they going to get the numerical superiority which they had in the autumn of 1916 and the spring of 1917, and which was then found not to be sufficient? What more can artillery do in offence than it has already done in the great battles of this year and last? What grounds are there for supposing that we possess more staying power or more national discipline than the Germans? What more is to be looked for from the blockade? If there is an alternative plan let us have it. If not, let this one have its fair chance. Let it be backed with as good an effort as was given to the creation of the British artillery in 1915 and 1916. Let other interests be made to concede and conform to its essential requirements. Surely we ought to have a plan for which we can strive, and not simply go carrying on from day to day and from hand to mouth in the hopes of something turning up before we reach the final abyss of general anarchy and world famine.

16. There is a short way of ending this war: it is to defeat

the German armies in the West. For this purpose two conditions are necessary: first, we must have stronger and better armies ourselves: that is the foundation on which everything rests, and there is no reason why we should not have it in 1919. Secondly we must discover a method of the offensive which enables these stronger armies to advance at a certain moderate rate of progression along their selected strategical lines. The problem is therefore definite and precise. Indeed it is mainly mechanical. Discover a method by which a stronger army can regain its rightful power of continuous advance, and decisive victory is won. It is mechanical methods which are preventing that advance. Overcome these by mechanical agency, and courage and quality will once again receive their due.

III

17. There is one other aspect of the problem to which I referred in my paper of the 21st October last, namely the scale and intensity of a decisive conflict. War between equals in power is not an affair which can be carried to a result merely by quasi business and administrative processes flowing smoothly out month after month and year after year. It should be a succession of climaxes on which everything is staked, towards which everything tends, and from which permanent decisions are obtained. These climaxes have usually been called battles. A battle means that the whole resources on either side that can be brought to bear are during the course of a single episode concentrated upon the enemy. There has not been a battle in this war since the battle of the Marne of which this could be said. We in England particularly are misled by the increasing scale of our casualties, due to the increasing size of our armies, into thinking that the intensity of the conflict is greater now than in the opening stages of the war. The battle of the Somme in the period of its greatest fury involved no more than the engagement simultaneously of about twenty British and French divisions against probably half that number of Germans; and the battle of Verdun ceased when the battle of the Somme had begun. All the great operations of 1916 and 1917, although so prolonged as to cause very heavy losses, have involved the

simultaneous employment only of comparatively small forces on comparatively small fronts. The armies have been fighting in instalments; they have engaged perhaps 8 or 10 per cent of their total strength.

18. The reasons which have led to this are well known. The power of the defensive is such that practically the whole spare artillery of an army has to be collected to support a single attack in which there is no room for more than a tenth of the available troops. There has never been, and there will never be, enough artillery to enable, say, six battles of Messines to be fought at one and the same moment. And thus the war in the West has dwindled down to siege operations on a gigantic scale which however bloody and prolonged cannot yield a decisive result. Thus, when a great battle is raging on the British front, six or eight British divisions are fighting desperately, half a dozen others are waiting to sustain them, the rest of the front is calm; twenty British divisions are remaining quietly in their trenches doing their daily routine, another twenty are training behind the lines; 20,000 men are at school, 10,000 are playing football, 100,000 are on leave. It is the same with the enemy. Obviously we have passed out of the region where the scale and intensity of the operations can be decisive on the great armies which are in presence of each other. Still less can they be decisive on the great belligerent nations. The idea of ending the war by 'killing Germans' is a delusion. You have got to kill or totally incapacitate at least 700,000 Germans in every year, *i. e.*, a number equal to the annual increment, before the slightest progress is made towards wearing down their manhood. And it takes at least one man's life to kill a German. We have to be, in short, merely exchanging lives, and exchanging lives upon a scale at once more frightful than anything that has been witnessed before in the world, and too modest to produce a decision.

19. Contrast this with the first two shocks of the war in the West, namely the first collision on the frontiers or the supreme struggle at the Marne. In the first three weeks of the war, between the 20th August and the 10th or 12th September, the whole of the French and German armies, every division, every available man, were simultaneously, continuously, or repeatedly engaged in open and moving warfare.

CHAPTER XVII

THE TWENTY-FIRST OF MARCH

The German Peace Opportunity—Ludendorff's Power—'Michael' and 'Mars'—Hindenburg's Order—At the British Headquarters—The Commander-in-Chief's Anxieties—With the 9th Division—The Barrage Falls—The Scale of the Battle—The First Day—The Battle Zone—Stubborn Resistance of the British Infantry—The Germans Cross the Somme—'Mars'—French Assistance—The Last Phase—Ludendorff's Strategic Failure—Where the Blame Lies—In Whitehall—The Doullens Meeting—General Gough—His Supersession—The Munition Workers' Achievement—The Guns Replaced.

AS the Paschendale struggle died away in the storms and mud of winter, the military rulers of Germany addressed themselves to a new situation. The collapse of Russia had enabled them to transport 1,000,000 men and 3,000 guns from the Eastern to the Western Front. For the first time therefore since the invasion they found themselves possessed of a definite superiority over the Allies in France. But this superiority was fleeting. The United States had declared war and was arming, but had not yet arrived. Once the great masses of American manhood could be trained, equipped, transported and brought into the line of battle, all the numerical advantage Germany had gained from the destruction of Russia would be more than counterbalanced. At the same time the German Main Headquarters knew the grave losses the British Army had suffered at Paschendale, and felt themselves entitled to count upon a marked decline in its strength and fighting quality. Lastly, the amazing character of the German-Austrian victory over the Italians at Caporetto glittered temptingly.

This was undoubtedly a favourable opportunity for peace negotiations. Russia down, Italy gasping, France exhausted, the British armies bled white, the U-boats not yet defeated, and the United States 3,000 miles away, constituted cumulatively a position where German statesmanship might well have intervened decisively. The immense conquests which Germany had made in Russia, and the hatred and scorn with which the Bolsheviks were regarded by the Allies, might well have made it possible for Germany to make important territorial concessions to France, and to offer Britain the complete restoration of Belgium. The desertion by Soviet Russia of the Allied cause, and the consequent elimination of all Russian claims, created a similar easement in negotiations for both Austria and Turkey. Such were the elements of this great opportunity. It was the last.

But Ludendorff cared for none of these things. We must regard him at this juncture as the dominating will. Since the fall of Bethmann-Hollweg, he and Hindenburg, at the head of the German General Staff machine, had usurped, or at least acquired, the main control over policy. The Emperor, inwardly appalled by the tide of events, suspected of being a pacifist at heart, failed increasingly to play his part. Thus on definite trials of strength the military power proved repeatedly to be predominant. It stood on the specialised basis of military opinion, not capable of measuring justly many of the most important forces which were at work internally and abroad. It was all the more dangerous because it was not complete. Ludendorff and Hindenburg by threatening resignation could obtain the crucial decisions they desired. These decisions governed the fate of Germany. But they were only acquainted with a portion of the problem, and they could only carry out such parts of the indispensable resultant policy as fell within their own military sphere. There was altogether lacking that supreme combination of the King-Warrior-Statesman which is apparent in the persons of the great conquerors of history.

Ludendorff was bent on keeping Courland, Lithuania, and

Poland in the east. Had his own fame not been gained in
these regions? He was also determined to keep a part of
Belgium, including Liège, where he had also distinguished
himself. This he felt was imperative if the German armies
were to obtain a good strategic starting-point for a future
war. So far from ceding any portion of Alsace and Lorraine,
he and the General Staff regarded the acquisition of a pro-
tective zone west of Metz, including the Briey Basin, as a
bare measure of prudence. These postulates and the possession of the new armies regathered from the Russian front
settled the course of events.

On November 11, 1917, a day in the calendar afterwards
celebrated for other reasons, Ludendorff, von Kuhl and von
der Schulenberg met at Mons. The nominal masters of these
great Staff Officers—Hindenburg, Prince Rupprecht and the
Crown Prince—were not troubled to attend. The basis of the
conference was that there should be a supreme offensive in
the West; that there would only be enough troops for one
such offensive without any diversion elsewhere; that the offensive must be made in February or the beginning of March
before the Americans could develop their strength; and finally,
that it was the British Army which must be beaten. Various
alternative schemes were discussed and orders given for their
detailed preparation. Each received its code name. Von
Kuhl's plan of an attack against the front La Bassée-Armen-
tières was 'St. George I'; an attack on the Ypres salient, 'St.
George II'; one on Arras-Notre Dame de Lorette, 'Mars.'
Lastly, there were the 'Michaels' I, II and III. It was not
until January 24, after profound detailed study, that the
choice was finally made in favour of the 'Michaels.'

The objective of this attack was to break through the
Allied front and reach the Somme from Ham to Péronne. The
date originally fixed was March 20. The battle was to be
extended by the attack 'Mars South' a few days later, and
a subsidiary attack, called 'Archangel,' by the Seventh Army

south of the Oise was to be used as a diversion. Preparations
for both the 'St. Georges' were also to be completed by the
beginning of April. Sixty-two divisions were available for the
three 'Michaels' and 'Mars South,' viz. Seventeenth Army:
fifteen attack divisions, two ordinary divisions; Second Army:
fifteen attack divisions, three ordinary divisions; Eighteenth
Army: nineteen attack divisions, five ordinary divisions; Reserve: three attack divisions. In spite of some differences of
opinion with von der Schulenberg and with von Hutier as to
the direction and emphasis of the offensive in its various stages,
Ludendorff adhered to his own conception: 'The British must
be beaten.' They could best be beaten by the attack on either
side of St. Quentin biting off the Cambrai salient. The Eighteenth Army would thereafter form a defensive flank along
the Somme to hold off the French, and all the rest of the
available German forces, wheeling as they advanced, were to
attack the British in a north-west direction and drive them
towards the coast. The two 'St. George' operations remained
in hand as further and potentially final blows. On these
foundations all the German armies concerned perfected their
arrangements.

Finally on March 10 the Emperor approved the following
order:—

CHIEF OF THE GENERAL STAFF.

Great Headquarters 10.3, issued 12.3.

His Majesty commands:
(1) That the Michael Attack take place on 21st March.
First penetration of the hostile position 9.40 a.m.
(2) The first great tactical objective of Crown Prince Rupprecht's Group of Armies will be to cut off the British in the
Cambrai salient and, north of the river Omignon and as far
as the junction of that river with the Somme, to capture the
line of Croisilles-Bapaume-Péronne. . . . Should the progress
of the attack by the right wing be very favourable it will push
on beyond Croisilles. The subsequent task of the Group of

Armies will be to push on towards Arras-Albert, left wing fixed on the Somme near Péronne, and with the main weight of the attack on the right flank to shake the English front opposite Sixth Army and to liberate further German forces from their stationary warfare for the advance. All divisions in rear of Fourth and Sixth Armies are to be brought forward forthwith in case of such an event.

(3) The German Crown Prince's Group of Armies is first of all to capture the Somme and Crozat Canal south of river Omignon. By advancing rapidly the Eighteenth Army must seize the crossings over the Somme and over the Canal. It must also be prepared to extend its right flank as far as Péronne. The Group of Armies will study the question of reinforcing the left wing of the Army by divisions from Seventh, First and Third Armies.

(4) O.H.L.[1] keeps control of 2nd Guard, 26th Württemberg and 12th Divisions.

(5) O.H.L. reserves its decision as regards Mars and Archangel, and will be guided by the course of events. Preparations for these are to be carried on uninterruptedly.

(6) The remaining Armies are to act in accordance with C.G.S. Operation Order 6925, dated 4th March. Rupprecht's Group of Armies will protect the right wing of the Mars-Michael operation against an English counter-attack. The German Crown Prince's Group of Armies will withdraw before any big attack by the French against Seventh (exclusive of Archangel front), Third and First Armies.

O.H.L. reserves its decision as regards the Groups of Armies of Gallwitz and Duke Albrecht concerning the strategic measures to be taken in the event of a big attack by the French or concerning the further withdrawal of divisions for the battle zone.

VON HINDENBURG.

Accompanied by the Master-General of the Ordnance, on March 19 I held a conference in the Armoury at Montreuil with the Chief of the Staff, the head of the Tank Corps, and a number of officers and experts, to settle the scheme of the Tank programme for 1919, and to time and organise the deliveries of tanks in 1918. I stayed with the Commander-in-

[1] Main Headquarters.

Chief. After luncheon Sir Douglas Haig took me into his private room and explained on his map the situation as he viewed it. The enormous German concentration on the British front, and particularly opposite the Fifth Army was obvious. Though nothing was certain, the Commander-in-Chief was daily expecting an attack of the first magnitude. The enemy masses in the north made it possible that the British front from Ypres to Messines would be assaulted. But the main developments were clearly to be expected on the sectors of the front from Arras to Péronne and even farther south. All these possibilities had already been amplified to me the day before by General Birch, the Chief of Artillery. His map showed very clearly the areas which the Germans were infecting with mustard gas (presumably to forbid them as manœuvring grounds to both sides for some days) and the wide gaps between these areas over which no doubt the hostile offensive would be launched. There were also heavy enemy concentrations, though less pronounced, against the French in the sector of the Aisne. Speaking generally, more than half the German divisions in the west were ranged against the front of the British armies; and over broad stretches, the estimated enemy rifle power, the most significant index, was four times what it was against the French.

The Commander-in-Chief viewed the coming shock with an anxious but resolute eye. He dwelt with insistence on the undue strain put upon his armies by the arrangement made by the War Cabinet with the French, in which he had reluctantly acquiesced, for the extension of the British front so far to the south as Barisis. He also complained of the pressure put upon him in such a situation to assign a large portion of his limited forces to the general reserve. His forces were inadequate for even sectional and G.H.Q. Reserves. How could he then find troops for a General Reserve? I suggested that if, as he believed, the enemy's main weight were to be thrown against the British, he would get the benefit of the whole of this reserve; and if not, *caderet quæstio*. To this he said he preferred the arrangements he had made with General Pétain, by which seven or eight British or French divisions were to be held ready to move laterally north or south according as the French or British should be found to be the object of the attack. From a general survey of the front it appeared that 110 German divisions faced 57 British, of which at least 40 German divisions faced our Fifth Army; that 85 German divisions faced 95 French; and that 4 German divisions faced the first 9 American divisions which had entered the line at various points, but particularly in the neighbourhood of St. Mihiel.

Our conversation ended about three o'clock. When I came out, the Master-General of the Ordnance suggested to me that as I had two days to spare before beginning the Chemical Warfare Conference at St. Omer, we should pay a flying visit to our old division, the 9th, which I had served in while it was in his charge, and which was now commanded by General Tudor, a friend of mine since subaltern days in India. We set off forthwith. General Tudor's headquarters were at Nurlu, in the devastated region ten miles to the north of Péronne, near the salient of the British line and in the centre of the threatened front. We received a hearty welcome when we arrived after dark upon a tranquil front lit rarely by a gun-flash.

General Tudor was in high expectation. Everything was in readiness. 'When do you think it will come?' we asked. 'Perhaps to-morrow morning. Perhaps the day after. Perhaps the week after.' We spent the whole of the next day in the trenches. A deathly and suspicious silence brooded over the front. For hours not a cannon shot was fired. Yet the sunlit fields were instinct with foreboding. The 9th Division were holding what they called 'The Disaster Front,' *i.e.* where the line had been stabilised after the successful German counter-stroke following the Battle of Cambrai. We examined every part of the defences from Gauche Wood, held by the gallant South Africans, the 'Springboks' as they were called, to the medium artillery positions on the slopes behind Havrincourt village. Certainly nothing that human thought and effort could accomplish had been neglected. For four miles in depth the front was a labyrinth of wire and scientifically sited machine-gun nests. The troops, though thin on the ground, were disposed so as to secure full value from every man. Rumours and reasonable expectations that the Germans would employ large numbers of tanks had led to the construction of broad minefields studded with buried shells with sensitive fuses amid wire entanglements. Through the narrow paths across these areas we picked our way gingerly. The sun was setting as we left Gauche Wood and took our leave of the South Africans. I see them now, serene as the Spartans of Leonidas on the eve of Thermopylæ.

Before I went to my bed in the ruins of Nurlu, Tudor said to me: 'It is certainly coming now. Trench raids this evening have identified no less than eight enemy battalions on a single half-mile of the front.' The night was quiet except for a rumble of artillery fire, mostly distant, and the thudding explosions of occasional aeroplane raids. I woke up in a complete silence at a few minutes past four and lay musing. Suddenly, after what seemed about half an hour, the silence was broken by six or seven very loud and very heavy explosions several miles away. I thought they were our 12-inch guns, but they were probably mines. And then, exactly as a pianist runs his hands across the keyboard from treble to bass, there rose in less than one minute the most tremendous cannonade I shall ever hear. 'At 4.30 a.m.,' says Ludendorff in his account, 'our barrage came down with a crash.' Far away, both to the north and to the south, the intense roar and reverberation rolled upwards to us, while through the chinks in the carefully papered window the flame of the bombardment lit like flickering firelight my tiny cabin.

I dressed and went out. On the duckboards outside the

Mess I met Tudor. 'This is *it*,' he said. 'I have ordered all our batteries to open. You will hear them in a minute.' But the crash of the German shells bursting on our trench lines eight thousand yards away was so overpowering that the accession to the tumult of nearly two hundred guns firing from much nearer to us could not be even distinguished. From the Divisional Headquarters on the high ground of Nurlu one could see the front line for many miles. It swept around us in a wide curve of red leaping flame stretching to the north far along the front of the Third Army, as well as of the Fifth Army on the south, and quite unending in either direction. There were still two hours to daylight, and the enormous explosions of the shells upon our trenches seemed almost to touch each other, with hardly an interval in space or time. Among the bursting shells there rose at intervals, but almost continually, the much larger flames of exploding magazines. The weight and intensity of the bombardment surpassed anything which anyone had ever known before.

Only one gun was firing at the Headquarters. He belonged to the variety called 'Percy,' and all his shells fell harmlessly a hundred yards away. A quarter of a mile to the south along the Péronne road a much heavier gun was demolishing the divisional canteen. Daylight supervened on pandemonium, and the flame picture pulsated under a pall of smoke from which great fountains of the exploding 'dumps' rose mushroom-headed. It was my duty to leave these scenes; and at ten o'clock, with mingled emotions, I bade my friends farewell and motored without misadventure along the road to Péronne. The impression I had of Tudor was of an iron peg hammered into the frozen ground, immovable. And so indeed it proved. The 9th Division held not only its Battle but its Forward Zone at the junction of the Third and Fifth Armies against every assault, and only retired when ordered to do so in consequence of the general movement of the line.

*   *   *   *   *

It is possible here to give only the barest outline of the battle. Many full and excellent accounts exist. Many more will be written. Taking its scale and intensity together, quantity and quality combined, 'Michael' must be regarded without exception as the greatest onslaught in the history of the world. From the Sensée River to the Oise, on a front of forty miles, the Germans launched simultaneously thirty-seven divisions of infantry, covered by nearly 6,000 guns. They held in close support nearly thirty divisions more. On the same front the British line of battle was held by seventeen divisions and 2,500 guns, with five divisions in support. There was in addition an attack south of the Oise by three German divisions against one British. In all the Germans had marshalled and set in motion rather more than three-quarters of a million men against 300,000 British. Over the two ten-mile sectors lying to the north and the south of the salient in which the 9th Division stood, the density of the enemy's formation provided an assaulting division for every thousand yards of ground, and attained the superiority of four to one.

The British troops involved constituted the whole of the Fifth and nearly half the Third Army under the command of General Gough and General Byng respectively. The system of defence comprised a Forward Zone intended to delay the enemy and to break his formations, and a Battle Zone in which the main struggle was to be fought. The average depth of the defensive system was about four miles; behind which again lay a Reserve Zone which there had not been time or labour to fortify, except for the defences of the medium and heavy batteries. Indeed, on the whole of the Fifth Army front, but especially in the newly-transferred sector from the Omignon to Barisis, many of the entrenched lines and points existed only in a rudimentary form. The rear zone, for instance, had a mere line a few inches deep cut in the turf, and communications in the shape of good roads and light railways were still lacking. The method of defence consisted in an intricate arrangement of small posts, machine-gun nests, and redoubts, mutually supporting each other, communicating with each other where necessary by trenches and tunnels, and covered or sustained by an exact organisation of artillery barrages. Behind the front of the British lay the wilderness of the Somme battlefield. Their left hand rested in a strategic sense upon the massive buttress of the Vimy Ridge; their right was in touch with comparatively weak French forces.

There was no surprise about the time or general direction of the attack. The surprise consisted in its weight, scale and power.

After a bombardment of incredible fury for not more than two to four hours, accompanied at certain points by heavy discharges of poison gas, the German infantry began to advance. The whole of this region had been in their possession during 1915 and the greater part of 1916, and there was no lack in any unit of officers and men who knew every inch of the ground. The form of attack which they adopted was an extension of the method of 'infiltration' first tried by them in their counter-stroke after the Battle of Cambrai. A low-lying fog, which was in some places dense, favoured their plan at any rate in the initial stages. The system of detached posts on which the British relied and which their comparatively small numbers had made necessarily rather open in character, depended to a very large extent upon clear vision, both for the machine gunners themselves and to a lesser extent for their protecting artillery. Aided by the mist, the German infantry freely entered the Forward Zone in small parties of shock troops, carrying with them machine guns and trench mortars. They were followed by large bodies, and even by noon had at many points penetrated the Battle Zone. The British posts, blasted, stunned or stifled by the bombardment or the gas, mystified and baffled by the fog, isolated and often taken in the rear, defended themselves stubbornly and with varying fortunes. Over the whole of the battlefield, which comprised

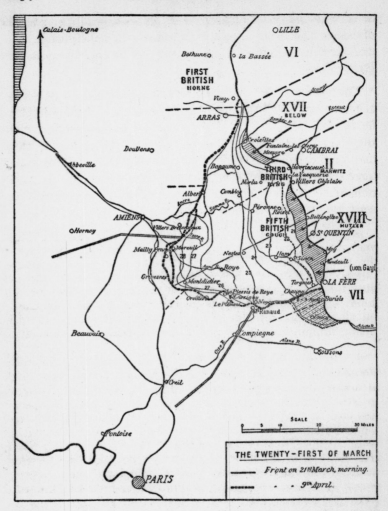

THE TWENTY-FIRST OF MARCH

———— Front on 21st March, morning.
-·-·-·-·- 9th April.

approximately 160 square miles, a vast number of bloody
struggles ensued. But the Germans, guided by their excellent
organisation and their local knowledge, and backed by their
immense superiority in numbers, continued during the day
to make inroads upon the Battle Zone, and even to pierce it

at several points. When darkness fell nearly all the British divisions had been forced from their original fighting line, and were intermingled at many points with the enemy in the Battle Zone.

The devoted resistance of the isolated British posts levied a heavy toll upon the enemy and played a recognisable part in the final result. From the outset the Germans learned that they had to deal with troops who would fight as long as they had ammunition, irrespective of what happened in any other quarter of the field or whether any hope of success or escape remained. A few instances of these forlorn struggles may record the glories of a hundred.

A platoon of the 2nd London (58th Division) holding Travecy Keep, north of La Fère, was entirely cut off in the morning and constantly attacked. All through the 21st they maintained themselves. They repulsed three heavy attacks at dusk on the 21st, at dawn on the 22nd and at midday on the 22nd. It was not until 5.30 p.m. on the 22nd that this handful of men, alone in the midst of the hostile army and with their ammunition running short, were compelled to surrender.

A company of the 7th Buffs (18th Division) garrisoned Vendeuil Fort in the same neighbourhood. They were first attacked about 9.45 a.m. on the 21st. The Germans advanced in close formation, and their attack was repulsed with great loss and the capture of some prisoners. The enemy then advanced past the fort in the fog, and its defenders knew they were cut off. Both in the evening of the 21st and after bombardment with field guns at dawn on the 22nd, the German attacks were again repulsed. During the 22nd this company was able to fire on long columns of cavalry, guns and transport passing their fort, and to drive them from the line of march. Not until 4.30 p.m. on the 22nd, when food and ammunition were both exhausted and there was no hope of relief, did they surrender.

On March 22nd Ricardo Redoubt, near Fontaine-les-Clercs (8 miles north-east of Ham), was held by the remains of the

1st Royal Inniskilling Fusiliers (36th Division), in all 275 officers and men. During the morning the place was surrounded and repeatedly attacked. About 2 p.m. the Germans brought up field artillery and bombarded the redoubt at close range. About an hour later the enemy gained a footing in the redoubt, and the struggle was continued inside. The Commanding Officer was now wounded, but it was not until 4.40 p.m. that the garrison was crushed after what the history of the German 3rd Guard Regiment describes as 'a most gallant resistance.'

On the 21st the headquarters and two companies of the 8th Queen's (24th Division) held the village of Le Verguier, seven miles north-west of St. Quentin, in the Battle Zone. During the day heavy frontal and flank attacks were made by the enemy, but all were repulsed. Greatly superior numbers of the enemy lay dead in the wire entanglements. No progress could be made by the Germans in this quarter. At 6.30 a.m. on the 22nd, aided by the morning mist, the enemy renewed his attack. The attack from the east by the German 185th Regiment failed. But the 5th German Guards, attacking from the north, succeeded in penetrating the side of the village and took in rear the defenders of the east face. The eastern part of the village was thus lost; but Fort Greathead and Fort Lees, as these small posts were called, on the western outskirts still held out. All men who could retire from the other posts reinforced these two, and thus strengthened they continued to repulse repeated attacks. The battalion headquarters in a sunken road south of the village was then discovered and attacked by the enemy. Orderlies, servants and cooks were quickly collected, and a spirited fight at close quarters ensued. The Germans were driven off.

About 9.30 a.m. the Commanding Officer went towards Fort Lees, the more northerly of the two posts, and found it had been lost. The remainder of the battalion was now nearly surrounded, and orders were given to retire. The defenders of Fort Greathead and of the battalion headquarters assembled in the sunken road leading southwestward from the village, and under cover of the mist marched off and rejoined their division with only one further casualty. They had defended Le Verguier for twenty-four hours, and its ruins with their

last defenders were taken by converging attacks made by
five German battalions from north, east and south, supported
by all the available artillery of two divisions.

On the 22nd one company of the 11th Royal Scots (9th
Division) was holding Revelon Farm, near Heudicourt (9
miles north-east of Péronne). During the afternoon Heudicourt Station, to the south of Revelon Farm, was taken by
the enemy. This enabled him to advance on the farm from
the south as well as from the east. The British record can
carry the tale no further than that the company of the Royal
Scots were last seen fighting hard for their farm at 5 p.m.
German accounts however testify to their defence. Bombarded at close range by artillery and trench mortars, bombed
by aeroplanes, and kept under ceaseless streams of machine-
gun bullets, the survivors resisted to the uttermost; and it was
nearly 6 o'clock when parts of three different German regiments stormed the farm. In the soldierly words of the history
of the German 123rd Regiment, 'they covered the retreat of
the main body to the extent of being destroyed themselves.'

The conflict was continuous. Fresh German troops poured
ceaselessly into action. By the evening of the 22nd the British Fifth Army had been driven completely beyond its battle
zone and half the Army was beyond its last prescribed defensive line. The British Third Army still fought in and around
the battle zone. The German penetration south of the Oise
had made serious progress. The British losses by death,
wounds or capture exceeded 100,000 men; and nearly 500
guns were already lost. An immense slaughter was also
wrought upon the German side. At every step they paid the
price of the offensive, but their great numbers rendered their
losses inappreciable during the crisis. Overwhelming reserves
were close at hand. The British on the other hand had only
eight divisions in general reserve, of which five were readily
available; and the French were too slowly moved or too far
away to give effective assistance for several days. Therefore
on the night of the 22nd, Sir Hubert Gough ordered a general
retreat of the Fifth Army behind the Somme. His orders had

been 'to protect at all costs the important centre of Péronne and the River Somme to the South' of it. He was fully justified in retiring in a general rear-guard action up to this line. But once the retreat of so thin a line on such a wide front had begun, it was very difficult to stop as long as the enemy pressure continued. The circumstances of each corps or division were so various that those who made a stand found their flanks exposed by others falling back. A great many of the bridges across the Somme were blown up; but enough were left—and among them the most important bridges, confided to the Railway authorities and not to the troops—to enable the Germans to pass artillery rapidly across. Moreover, the river was easily fordable at this time.

Backward then across the hideous desolation of the old crater-fields rolled the British front for five days in succession. The Cavalry Corps filled the gaps in the line, and the Air Force, concentrating all its strength upon the battle, flying low, inflicted heavy losses on the endless marching columns. Meanwhile reserves drawn from other parts of the line, and improvised forces from the schools and technical establishments, continually reached the scene. At the same time, with every day's advance, the strength and momentum of the German thrust abated. The actual fighting gave place to the painful toiling westward of two weary armies; and when the retreating British were sufficiently reinforced to come to a general halt, their pursuers found themselves not less exhausted, and far in front of their own artillery and supplies. By the evening of the 27th the first crisis of the great battle was over.

All the 'Michaels' had struck their blow. But where was 'Mars'? The Sixth Army and the right of the Seventeenth were to have entered the battle towards Arras and the Vimy Ridge on the 23rd. That they did not attack till the 28th was due to a deeply significant cause. General Byng had secretly withdrawn his troops from the line at Monchy, and already occupied a position four miles in the rear. The Ger-

mans bombarded the empty trenches of a false front. It took
them four days and nights to bring their artillery forward and
mount the assault against the new position. Thus the second
great wave did not synchronise with the full surge of the first.
The second great battle did not contribute to the intensity
of the first, but came as a separate event after the climax of
the first was over. Moreover, the progress made by the Second and the Seventeenth German Armies in the original attack had not fulfilled Ludendorff's expectations. At 9.30 on
the morning of the 23rd, he was led to abandon his prime
strategic hope, namely the general defeat and driving to the
coast of the British armies in France, and to content himself
with the extremely valuable definite objective of dividing
the British from the French through the capture of Amiens
towards which the Eighteenth and Second Armies were pro-
gressing. His order given at noon was: 'A considerable portion of the British Army has now been beaten. . . . The
objective of the operation is now to separate the French and
British by a rapid advance on both sides of the Somme.'
This was already a remarkable contraction of aim.

On the morning of the 28th the delayed attack against the
Arras position (Mars) began. It was delivered on a twenty-
mile front by twenty German divisions against eight British
divisions. The methods of both sides were the same as on
March 21. But the weather was clear, and the machine guns
and artillery of the defence could reach their highest concert.
Everywhere the attack was repulsed with tremendous slaughter. Even the Forward Zone was held at many points. No-
where was the Battle Zone seriously affected. No outside reserves were required by the defending divisions. The Germans, who advanced with the utmost bravery, were mown
down in heaps.[1] As the result of the eight days' struggle the

[1] 'It would almost seem,' says Sir Douglas Haig's Staff Officer, 'as
if the only difference numbers in the attack make to a properly located
machine-gun defence, when there is light and time to see, is to provide
a better target.' No one can quarrel with such a conclusion.

British Army, virtually unaided by the French, had stemmed or broken the greatest offensive ever launched.

The French had been coming fitfully and feebly into action on the Southern portion of the battlefield from the morning of the 23rd. At dawn that day one division (the 125th) came into action. A French dismounted cavalry division entered the line in the evening. The 9th, 10th, 62nd and 22nd French Divisions were in line on the afternoon of the 24th, though two of them had no artillery and none of them had 'cookers' or more than fifty rounds of rifle ammunition per man. On the morning of the 25th General Fayolle assumed responsibility for the whole of the Fifth Army front south of the Somme. But up till the 27th the main weight of the fighting, even in this area, still continued to be borne by the exhausted British troops. At no time up till the end of the 28th, when both the first and second crises of the battle were over, did the French have simultaneously in action more than six divisions, and none of these were seriously engaged. The struggle up till its turning point on the 28th was between the British and Germans alone.

Its last phase was now at hand, and in this the ever-gathering strength of the French on those portions of the front still involved played an equal part with the British. The Eighteenth German Army, brushing back weak French resistance, had actually taken Montdidier on the 27th. But this was the farthest point of the German advance. Says Ludendorff: 'The enemy's line was now becoming denser, and in places they were even attacking themselves; while our armies were no longer strong enough to overcome them unaided. The ammunition was not sufficient, and supply became difficult. The repair of roads and railways was taking too long, in spite of all our preparations. After thoroughly replenishing ammunition, the Eighteenth Army attacked between Montdidier and Noyon on March 30. On April 4 the Second Army and the right wing of the Eighteenth attacked at Albert, south of

the Somme towards Amiens. These actions were *indecisive*.[1]
It was an established fact that the enemy's resistance was
beyond our strength. . . . The battle was over by April 4.'

Let us focus what had actually happened. With whom lay
the victory? Contrary to the generally accepted verdict, I
hold that the Germans, judged by the hard test of gains and
losses, were decisively defeated. Ludendorff failed to achieve
a single strategic object. By the morning of the 23rd he had
been forced to resign his dream of overwhelming and crump-
ling back upon the sea the main strength of the British armies,
and to content himself with the hope of capturing Amiens
and perhaps dividing the British from the French. After
April 4 he abandoned both these most important but to him
secondary aims. 'Strategically,' he says, 'we had not achieved
what the events of the 23rd, 24th and 25th had encouraged
us to hope for. That we had also failed to take Amiens . . .
was specially disappointing.' What then had been gained?
The Germans had reoccupied their old battlefields and the
regions they had so cruelly devastated and ruined a year before. Once again they entered into possession of those grisly
trophies. No fertile province, no wealthy cities, no river or
mountain barrier, no new untapped resources were their reward. Only the crater-fields extending abominably where-
ever the eye could turn. The old trenches, the vast grave-
yards, the skeletons, the blasted trees and the pulverised villages—these, from Arras to Montdidier and from St. Quentin
to Villers-Bretonneux, were the Dead Sea fruits of the mighti-
est military conception and the most terrific onslaught which
the annals of war record. The price they paid was heavy.
They lost for the first time in the war, or at any rate since
Ypres in 1914, two soldiers killed for every one British, and
three officers killed for every two British. They made 60,000
prisoners and captured over a thousand guns, together with
great stores of ammunition and material. But their advan-

---

[1] My italics.

tage in prisoners was more than offset by their greater loss in wounded. Their consumption of material exceeded their captures. If the German loss of men was serious, the loss of time was fatal. The great effort had been made and had not succeeded. The German Army was no longer crouched, but sprawled. A great part of its reserves had been exposed and involved. The stress of peril on the other hand wrung from the Allies exertions and sacrifices which, as will be seen, far more than made good their losses.

The recriminations upon this battle left a lasting imprint on British political history. In April General Maurice, the Director at the War Office of Military Operations, indignant at the failure to reinforce the Army in the winter, accused Mr. Lloyd George of incorrectly stating to the House of Commons the facts and figures of the case. Tension and uncertainty arose not only in the Opposition, but among the Government supporters, and even in its own ranks. When a formal challenge in debate was made by Mr. Asquith, the Prime Minister convinced the House that his statement had been founded on information supplied in writing by General Maurice's Deputy. This was decisive on the issue, and the actual merits of the controversy were scarcely discussed. The division which followed was accepted by Mr. Lloyd George as marking the cleavage between his Liberal followers and those of Mr. Asquith. When, eight months later, in the hour of victory, the General Election took place, all who had voted against the Government on this occasion were opposed by the triumphant Coalition, and scarcely any escaped political exclusion. The reverberations of the quarrel continue to this day.

We may however attempt a provisional judgment. If Haig had not consumed his armies at Paschendale, or if at least he had been content to stop that offensive in September, he would have commanded (without any addition to the drafts actually sent him from England in the winter) sufficient reserves on March 21 to enable him to sustain the threatened front. But for the horror which Paschendale inspired in the minds of the Prime Minister and the War Cabinet, he would no doubt have been supplied with very much larger reinforcements. He would thus have gained both in economy of life and also in larger reinforcements. If, notwithstanding Paschendale, the War Cabinet had reinforced him as they should have done, the front could still have been held on March 21. The responsibility for the causes which led to the British inadequacy of numbers is shared between General Headquarters and the War Cabinet. By constitutional doctrine the greatest responsibility unquestionably rests upon the War Cabinet, who failed to make their Commander conform to their convictions on a question which far transcended the military or technical sphere, and who also failed to do full justice to the Army because of their disagreement with the Commander-in-Chief. In view however of the preponderance of military influence in time of war, and the serious dangers of a collision between the 'soldiers' and the politicians, a very considerable burden must be borne by the British Headquarters.

* * * * *

My work at the Chemical Warfare School near St. Omer occupied the whole of the 23rd, and I did not reach London till midday on the 24th. No information of any value about the progress of the battle had been available at the Chemical School. I therefore went immediately to the War Office to learn the news from France. Sir Henry Wilson, with the gravest face, showed me the telegrams and his own map. We both walked across to Downing Street, where the Prime Minister was expecting him. It was a bright crisp day, and Mr. Lloyd George was seated in the garden with Lord French. He seemed to think that I had news at first hand, and turned towards me. I explained that I knew nothing beyond what he had already read in his telegrams, and had seen nothing but the first few hours of the bombardment in a single sector. After some general conversation he took me aside and posed the following question: If we could not hold the line we had fortified so carefully, why should we be able to hold any positions farther back with troops already defeated? I answered that every offensive lost its force as it proceeded. It was like throwing a bucket of water over the floor. It first rushed forward, then soaked forward, and finally stopped altogether until another bucket could be brought. After thirty or forty miles there would certainly come a considerable breathing space, when the front could be reconstituted if every effort were made. It appeared that he had already despatched Lord Milner to France, though I was not aware of this. The Chief of the Staff said that he himself intended to go over that night. We arranged to dine together at my house in Eccleston Square before he left. Only my wife was present. I never remember in the whole course of the war a more anxious evening. One of the great qualities in Mr. Lloyd George was his power of obliterating the past and concentrating his whole being upon meeting the new situation. There were 200,000 troops in England that could be swiftly sent. What about munitions and equipment? Wilson said, 'We might well lose a thousand guns,' and that 'mountains of ammunition and stores of every kind must have been abandoned.' I was thankful to be in a position to say that about these at least there need be no worry. Everything could be replaced at once from our margins without affecting the regular supply. Presently the Chief of the General Staff went to catch his train, and we were left alone together. The resolution of the Prime Minister was unshaken under his truly awful responsibilities.

Meanwhile an event had occurred which, though it did not influence the course of the battle, was nevertheless of capital importance. On the night of the 24th, when the battle was at its worst, General Pétain, whose weak and tardy assistance was causing grave concern, met Haig and his Chief of Staff at Dury near Amiens. Although sixty-two German divisions had already been identified in the battle, of which forty-eight were fresh from the Reserve, Pétain asserted that the main blow was yet to fall, and that it would fall on the French in Champagne. He informed Haig that if the Germans continued to press on to Amiens, the French troops then concentrating about Montdidier would be withdrawn upon Beauvais to cover Paris in accordance with the orders of the French Government. He indicated that action in this sense had already been taken. Haig's original orders, given him personally by Lord Kitchener more than two years before, were in brief to 'keep united with the French Army at all costs.' But here at the crisis was a complete abandonment of the basic principle of unity.

On learning this fatal intention, Sir Douglas Haig telegraphed to the Secretary of State for War and the Chief of the Imperial General Staff to come over immediately. But both, as we have seen, had already started independently. Milner, acting with the necessary energy, after seeing Haig's Chief of the Staff at St. Omer, motored straight through to Paris and collected the President of the Republic, Clémenceau and Foch. Together they all proceeded to Compiègne on the 25th, examined Pétain as to his intentions, and finally, bringing Pétain with them, at noon on the 26th met Haig at Doullens, where Henry Wilson had already arrived. The magnitude of the danger had melted all prejudices and oppositions, personal and national alike. Only one name was in every mind. Foch, a week ago described as a 'dotard,' was the indispensable man. He alone possessed the size and the combative energy to prevent the severance of the French and British armies. Milner proposed that Foch should have control of the forces in front of Amiens. Haig declared that this was insufficient and that Foch must be given actual command of the French and British armies as a whole 'from the Alps to the North Sea.' At a conference in London a month before, the old 'Tiger' had dealt abruptly with the outspoken misgivings of Foch. 'Taisez-vous. I am the representative of France.' Now it was Foch's turn to speak. 'It is a hard task you offer me now: a compromised situation, a crumbling front, an adverse battle in full progress. Nevertheless I accept.' Thus there was established for the first time on the Western Front that unity of command towards which Mr. Lloyd George had long directed his cautious, devious but persevering steps, and to which, whatever may be said to the contrary (and it is not little), history will ascribe an inestimable advantage for the cause of the Allies.

The emergency arrangements were confirmed and elaborated a few weeks later in the so-called 'Beauvais Agreement' under which the Commander-in-Chief of a National Army was secured right of appeal to his own Government if he claimed that an order of the Generalissimo endangered the safety of his troops.

Hard measure was meted out to General Gough. The Fifth Army from the 28th onwards ceased to exist. Its shattered divisions were painfully reorganised behind the line. The gap was filled by the now rapidly arriving French, by the cavalry, by the improvised forces collected from the Schools, and by General Rawlinson who began, from scanty and diverse materials, to constitute a 'Fourth Army' and to maintain the tottering and fluctuating line of battle.

Gough never received another fighting command. The Cabinet insisted on his removal on the ground, probably valid, that he had lost the confidence of his troops. This officer had fought his way upwards through the whole war from a Cavalry Brigade to the command of an army. He was held to have greatly distinguished himself on the Ancre at the close of 1916. With Plumer he bore the brunt of Paschendale while it continued, and its blame when it ended rested upon him. He was a typical cavalry officer, with a strong personality and a gay and boyish charm of manner. A man who never spared himself or his troops, the instrument of costly and forlorn attacks, he emerged from the Paschendale tragedy pursued by many fierce resentments among his high subordinates, rumours of which had even reached the rank and file. For over a year his reputation had been such that troops and leaders alike disliked inclusion in the Fifth Army. There was a conviction that in that Army supplies were awkward and attacks not sufficiently studied. In these circumstances Gough was not in a position to surmount the impression of a great disaster. The sternest critic has however been unable to find ground for censuring his general conduct of the battle of March 21. It appears that he took every measure, both before and during the battle, which experience and energy could devise and of which his utterly inadequate resources admitted; that his composure never faltered, that his activity was inexhaustible, that his main decisions were prudent and resolute, and that no episode in his career was more honourable than the disaster which entailed his fall.

* * * * *

It was my responsibility to make good the assurance I had given that all losses in material would be immediately replaced; and for this the Munitions Council, its seventy departments and its two and a half million workers, men and women, toiled with a cold passion that knew no rest. Everywhere the long-strained factories rejected the Easter breathing space which health required. One thought dominated the whole gigantic organisation—to make everything good within a month. Guns, shells, rifles, ammunition, Maxim guns, Lewis guns, tanks, aeroplanes and a thousand ancillaries were all gathered from our jealously hoarded reserves. Risks are relative, and I decided, without subsequent misadventure, to secure an earlier month's supply of guns by omitting the usual firing tests.

On the 26th I issued the following notice:—

'A special effort must be made to replace promptly the serious losses in munitions which are resulting from the great battle now in progress. It should be our part in the struggle to maintain the armament and equipment of the fighting troops at the highest level. Our resources are fortunately sufficient to accomplish this up to the present in every class of munitions. But it is necessary to speed up the completion and despatch of important parts of the work in hand. I rely upon every one concerned in the manufacture of tanks to put forward their best efforts. There should therefore be no cessation of this work during the Easter holidays. Please notify your essential subcontractors to this effect.

'I acknowledge with gratitude the spontaneous assurances already received from the men in many districts that there will be no loss of output. Now is the time to show the fighting army what the industrial army can achieve.'

The response was so complete that explanations had to be offered a few days later to those who felt their work slighted because they had not been called upon to sacrifice their hard-earned holidays.

'The Minister of Munitions desires to acknowledge in the warmest terms the widespread and indeed general response which has been made from all parts of the country to the appeal to the munition workers to give up their Easter holidays. He would like to accept all the offers that have been made. But military and railway exigencies at this juncture make it necessary to confine acceptance to those classes of work particularly referred to in the Minister's appeal. All firms whose work must be specially accelerated have now been notified individually by official telegram that they should work through Easter. Those who have not been notified should take their holidays now. This will allow the railway facilities to be used to the highest advantage for the most urgent needs. It in no way implies that one class of munitions work is more important than another, and it is vital that all munition outputs should be increased to the maximum which material allows.'

Cui

C. The follow

a carriages

by April

England.

18 p

4 5"

60 p

6" H

6" S

Before the end of the month I was able, in the facsimile document on the opposite page, to assure the War Cabinet and General Headquarters that nearly two thousand new guns of every nature, with their complete equipments, could be supplied by April 6 as fast as they could be handled by the receiving department of the Army. In fact, however, twelve hundred met the need.

CHAPTER XVIII

THE CLIMAX

The Battle of the Lys, April 9—The Portuguese gap—The second wave—The buttresses stand—The battle is prolonged—The 'Back-to-the-wall' order—April 12, the Climax—Haig's Appeals to Foch —Reasons for Foch's obduracy—Munitions and Tanks—The King's Message to the Munition Workers—Two bleak hypotheses—My note of April 18—Tragic Contingencies—Loss of Kemmel Hill—The false alarm—Ludendorff flinches—Defeat and Losses of the Germans.

ON Tuesday, April 9, the third great battle effort of the Germans against the British began. In order to stem the German advance upon Amiens, Sir Douglas Haig had been forced to thin his line elsewhere. Instead of doing this evenly, he had exercised a wise process of selection. He held in strength the great central bastion from Arras to the La Bassée Canal at Givenchy. This comprised the highly defensible and important area of the Lens coalfields, as well as the mass of commanding ground which included the key positions of the Vimy and Lorette Heights. To the north of this it was inevitable that the line should be dangerously weak. Out of fifty-eight British infantry divisions, forty-six had already been engaged on the Somme. The Fifth Army divisions were reorganising and unfit to enter the line. To hold the front of 40,000 yards between the La Bassée Canal and the Ypres Canal, Haig could only provide six divisions. Each of these divisions must be stretched to cover over 7,000 yards— stretched wider, that is to say, than the Fifth Army divisions before March 21; and almost all the troops had fought with most severe losses in the preceding fortnight on the Somme. Since even these precarious dispositions could not be completed in the pressure of events before the German blow fell, nearly 10,000 yards of front by Neuve Chapelle were at the moment held by a Portuguese division of four brigades.

It was upon this denuded front, the day before the Portuguese were to have been relieved by two British divisions, that Ludendorff struck. By April 3, seventeen divisions had been added to the German Sixth and four to the German Fourth Army. The Sixth Army was to attack towards Hazebrouck and the heights beyond Kemmel, and the Fourth was to support it and exploit success. The town of Armentières, having been smothered with gas shells by a bombardment beginning on the evening of the 7th, constituted an impassable area; and with their northern flank thus protected, ten German divisions in an eleven-miles' line marched against the 2nd Portuguese Division and the 40th and 55th British Divisions on each side of it. No less than seven German divisions fell upon the four Portuguese brigades, and immediately swept them out of existence as a military force. The 40th Division, its flank opened by the Portuguese disaster, was also speedily overwhelmed. A thick mist blanketed the British machine-gun nests arranged in depth behind the line. Within two hours of the advance of the German infantry a gap of over 15,000 yards had been opened in the front, through which the German masses were pouring. The 50th and 51st Divisions, who formed the British reserves, moved to their appointed stations in the second line of defence at the crossings of the Lys and the Lawe Rivers as soon as the battle began; but the unexampled suddenness of the break-through, the vehemence of the German advance, the streams of retreating Portuguese, and the general confusion prevented them from fully occupying their prepared positions. They were rapidly absorbed in a moving battle against vastly superior numbers. After a day of violent fighting the Germans had reached the outskirts of Estaires, five kilometres behind the original line, and around this pocket of assault the remains of five British divisions

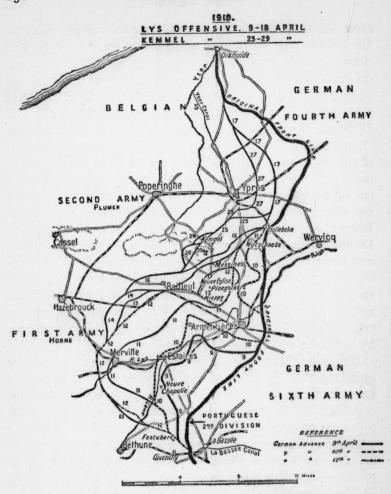

struggled to create and maintain a front against sixteen German divisions all fully engaged.

At daylight on the morning of the 10th a second wave of German assault was launched by the German Fourth Army to the north of Armentières on a four-mile front. This phase of the offensive had been timed to begin twenty-four hours

after the main attack, in the well-founded expectation that
the British reserves in this sector would by then have been
drawn into the first battle. Four brigades had in fact been
diverted, and the whole weight of five German divisions fell
upon five brigades of the 19th and 25th Divisions, who had
behind them in reserve only the remaining brigade of the 29th
Division. The assault was successful. The front was broken.
'Plugstreet' village, the greater part of Messines and the crest
of the Wytschaete Ridge fell into the hands of the enemy by
noon. The 34th Division was in the greatest danger of being
cut off around Armentières, and by the evening of the 10th
the Germans were actual or potential masters of the whole
British defensive system from Wytschaete to Givenchy.
During the day both Lestrem and Estaires had been taken,
and night found the survivors of eight British divisions holding an improvised front of thirty miles at death grips with
twenty-seven German divisions, of which twenty-one had
actually been involved in the battle. The 34th Division extricated itself from Armentières during the night, and only
by skill escaped the fast closing pincers.

But while this formidable inroad had been made upon the
greater part of the front assailed, the line on either flank held
firm. A Lancashire division, the 55th, perfectly fortified and
organised in Givenchy and Festubert, continued to repulse
for seven successive days every attack, losing 3,000 men and
taking 900 prisoners. On the northern flank of the offensive
lay the 9th Scottish Division whom we left unshakable at
Nurlu on the morning of March 21. After fighting with the
utmost distinction and success in that great battle and losing
over 5,000 officers and men, it had been hastily filled with
drafts and brought to rest and recuperate in what was believed to be a quiet station. The whole front to the south-
ward having been beaten in, its right flank was turned back;
and the resurrected South African brigade, at four in the
afternoon of the 10th, drove the Germans from the Messines

crest. All efforts to oust this division from the position into which it had clawed itself failed. Thus the buttresses stood immovable, although the wall between them was completely battered in. Upon this fact the safety of the whole front and the final result of the battle unquestionably depended.

On the 11th the enemy, his Sixth and Fourth Army fronts united, extended his inroads in every direction except the flanks which he could not widen. Villages and townships, which had for more than three years been the home of the British armies or whose names were associated with hard-won victories, fell into his hands. Merville, Nieppe and the rest of Messines were lost. As his front extended the enemy was able to deploy additional divisions and simultaneously to increase the weight of the attack and stretch the thin-drawn fluctuating line of the defence. The 50th and 51st Divisions maintained during the whole of April 10 and 11 a desperate struggle with seven or more German divisions along an oscillating but receding front of 20,000 yards.

By the end of this day the German line formed a salient or bulge fifteen kilometres deep and sixty-four wide in the original British positions. Meanwhile reinforcements were hurrying to the scene by march, bus and train. The rest of the 29th Division began to arrive on the northern front of attack, and the 4th, 5th, 31st (including the 4th Guards Brigade), 33rd, 61st and 1st Australian Divisions were all moving to the southern sector. Every yard of the ground was disputed, and in the close fierce fighting which never ceased night or day the German losses, like their numbers, were at least double those of the British. Here at last, though perilous, agonising and unrecognised, was the real battle of attrition.

The initial success of the German thrust had exceeded Ludendorff's expectations, and during the first forty-eight hours of the battle he formed the resolve to extend the scale of the attack and strike with all his strength for the Channel ports. From April 12 onwards the German reserves were

thrown profusely into the conflict, and both the German
Army Commanders, Quast and Sixt von Arnim, were encouraged to draw freely from the main concentrations in the north.
Begun as a diversion to draw Allied reserves from the Amiens
front, the Battle of the Lys had now become a primary operation.

*   *   *   *   *

From the general not less than from the British point of
view, April 12 is probably, after the Marne, the climax of
the war. It looked as if the Germans had resolved to stake
their fate and their regathered superiority on battering the
life out of the British Army. During twenty days they had
hurled nearly ninety divisions in three great battles upon an
army which counted no more than fifty-eight, and of these
nearly half were fastened to fronts not under attack. With
a superiority of numbers in the areas of assault of three and
often four to one, with their brilliantly trained shock troops,
with their extraordinary skill and enterprise in manœuvring
with machine guns and trench mortars, with their new infiltration scheme, with their corroding mustard gas, with their
terrific artillery and great science of war, they might well
succeed. The French seemed to the British Headquarters
sunk in stupor and passivity. Since the Nivelle disaster they
had been grappling with mutiny and nursing their remaining
resources. With the exception of the 'set piece' battle of
Malmaison in the winter, and the stinted and tardy divisions
which had been involved south of the Somme in the later
stages of March 21, they had only fought in ordinary trench
warfare for nearly nine months. During that time the much
smaller British Army had fought almost unceasingly, and
wisely or unwisely had sacrificed in the common cause, apart
from the prolonged Arras-Messines offensive of 1917, more
than 400,000 men in the Paschendale tragedy, and had now
lost nearly 300,000 more under Ludendorff's terrible hammer.
It was upon an Army bled white by frightful losses, its regi-

mental officers shorn away by scores of thousands, its batteries and battalions filled and refilled with young soldiers plunged into battle before they knew their officers or each other, that the massed might of the desperate German Empire now fell.

Moreover, the shock could not be deadened nor breathing space gained by ceding ground. No large retirement like the *Alberich* manœuvre was open to Sir Douglas Haig. A few kilometres might be yielded here and there. The dearly bought ground of Paschendale could be given up and some relief obtained thereby. Ypres could in the last resource be let go. But in front of Amiens, in front of Arras, in front of Béthune, in front of Hazebrouck he must stand or fall. Therefore on the morning of the 12th the Commander, usually so restrained and, as it had seemed, unresponsive, published to his troops the order of the day which is printed in facsimile on the opposite page: 'There is no other course open to us but to fight it out. Every position must be held to the last man. There must be no retirement. With our backs to the wall and believing in the justice of our cause, each one of us must fight on to the end.' All units and all ranks of the British Expeditionary Force therefore prepared themselves to conquer or die.

The convulsion continued. The reinforcements closed the gaps that were hourly torn in the struggling line. Companies, battalions, even whole brigades were obliterated where they stood. Ludendorff, resolute, ruthless, hazard-loving, raised his stakes. More and more of the German reserves were committed to the onset. The roar of the cannonade resounded through Flanders and reverberated across the Channel. But nothing could move the 55th Division on the right nor the 9th on the left. The Australians were coming, but their trains were late; and the 4th Guards Brigade all through the 12th and 13th may be discerned, where all was valour, barring the path to Hazebrouck. So intermingled were the units

Three weeks ago
tacks against us
eparation from th
d destroy the Bri
despite of throwing
~~suffering~~ endu
the loss as yet
We owe this to th
r troops. Words
el for the splendid
y under the most
many amongst
I would say th
ch holds out the
idly & in great
There is no other
! Every position
t be no retirem
believing in
must fight on
mes and the Fr
on the conduct
oment. But
t win in the
uvid my

and formations in the fighting line, that across the Bailleul-Armentières road, Freyberg, V.C., four years before a Sub-Lieutenant, found himself holding a front of 4,000 yards with elements of four different divisions, and covered by the remnants of two divisional artilleries that had drifted back with the line. Neuve Eglise was lost, and Bailleul and Méteren; and under the intense pressure the front bent backwards. But it did not break. When on the 17th eight German divisions—seven of them fresh—were violently repulsed in their attack on the famous hill of Kemmel, the crisis of the Battle of the Lys was over. The orders of the Commander had been strictly and faithfully fulfilled.

*   *   *   *   *

Even before the beginning of the Battle of the Lys Sir Douglas Haig had convinced himself that Ludendorff meant to make a dead-set at the British Army. He accordingly appealed to Foch for aid.

He asked the Generalissimo to take without delay one of the three following courses, viz.—

'(1) To open an offensive in the next five or six days with the French armies on a scale sufficient to attract the enemy's reserves, or

'(2) To relieve the British troops south of the Somme (a total of four divisions), or

(3) To place a group of four French divisions in the neighbourhood of St. Pol as a reserve to the British front.'

He wrote again on the 10th after the battle had begun that the—

'enemy would without a doubt continue to strike against his troops until they were exhausted. It was vital that the French Army should take immediate steps to relieve some part of the British front and take an active share in the battle.'

He renewed his solicitations on the 11th and on the 14th. Finally on the 15th he recorded his—

'opinion that the arrangements made by the Generalissimo were insufficient to meet the military situation.'

In order to press his demands with greater insistency, and withal to maintain good relations with the Supreme Commander, Haig, as early as April 10, had taken General Du Cane, who was actually commanding the XVth British Corps in full battle on the Lys, and sent him to reside at Foch's headquarters as a High 'Go-between' or Liaison Officer.

These requests were intensely painful to Foch. His primary endeavour was to gather and husband his reserves. The control exercised over the reserves was, he considered, the main function of a Commander on the defensive. Ten British divisions had already on account of their losses had to be reduced to cadre, and their survivors used as reinforcements for the rest. When could these divisions, he asked, be reconstituted? Could not the British when the crisis of the battle was over start a 'roulement' of tired British divisions to quiet parts of the French front? These counter requests ill accorded with the desperate struggle in which the British were involved. Painful differences developed at a conference held at Abbeville on April 14 between Foch and Haig, at which Lord Milner was present. Foch took the view that 'la bataille du Nord,' as he called it, was dying down, and that his reserves were suitably placed to intervene either in the Flanders battle or in the battle of Arras-Amiens-Montdidier, which he expected would be renewed at any moment. His attitude excited the resentment of the British representatives, and no agreement was reached. He had seen the 1st British Army Corps fight at Ypres in 1914; and the impression that British troops would stand any test if resolutely called upon was indelible.

It was no doubt the duty of Foch to hoard his reserves and to extort the fullest effort from every part of the Allied armies; but he was at least premature in his judgment that 'the battle in the North was dying down,' nor had he any right to count upon the intense resistance which was in the event forthcoming from the desperately pressed British troops. Foch's doctrine of never relieving troops during a battle may apply to a battle of two or three days; but struggles prolonged over weeks do not admit of such rules. Divisions after a certain point, if not relieved, simply disappear through slaughter and intermingling with the reinforcements who are sent to sustain them; and the individual survivors of many days of ceaseless peril, horror and concussion become numb and lifeless, even though unscathed by steel.

The British, Government and Headquarters alike, upon whose initiative Foch had just been raised to the supreme control, were already distrustful of the use he would make of his power. It must be conceded however that Foch was vindicated by the event, for the British armies weathered the storm practically unaided and the German impulsion gradually died away.

Slowly and reluctantly Foch was compelled to part with a small portion of his reserves and on April 18 a detachment from the French Army of the North (D.A.N.) consisting of five infantry and three cavalry divisions was formed to take over the front Bailleul-Wytschaete. These troops, however, even after they had arrived on the scene, only gradually came into the line. In the end this French force was raised to nine infantry divisions. But before then the crisis had passed.

*   *   *   *   *

We must descend from the immortal events of the battle-field to the thread of personal narrative which binds together this account. To many in the official circle the series of great battles which had filled these weeks presented the impression of one long frenzy. Men bent to their daily tasks for comfort. But my work kept me so closely in touch with the Army and its Chiefs that I could not fail to comprehend to

soldiers who are fighting supplied with all they need, and also of admiring the organising ability displayed in so many ways and on so great a scale. The King is deeply impressed by the fact that much-needed holidays should have been cheerfully given up, and additional exertions made, at a time when many severe food restrictions had come into force, and that in spite of large numbers of munition workers having left the workshops for the Army during the last six months, the outputs of every kind should not only have been maintained but steadily increased. Accordingly the King has directed the Minister to convey His Majesty's thanks to all concerned.'

*   *   *   *   *

But the continuance of the battle, the power of the enemy and the obvious jeopardy in which our army stood forced most grave reflections. Suppose the Germans continued tearing at our throats with all their might, suppose they shook the life out of our army, suppose the straining front broke or was swept back by an inexorable tide! There were at any rate 'the water lines.' The advanced line ran from Dunkirk back to the second or main line. This ran along the stream of the Aa from Gravelines through St. Omer to St. Venant. A vast amount of work had been done upon it. It was called 'the water line' on account of the great part which inundations could be made to play in its defence. This line would shorten the front and be a substantial relief, but it meant the loss of Dunkirk and the continuous bombardment of Calais. Both these ports played a notable part in the reception of our supplies, and far-reaching checks and complications would follow on their loss.

Even darker possibilities were afoot. Suppose we had to choose between giving up the Channel ports or being separated from the mass of the French armies! In the former case all our best and closest communications would be destroyed. We should have to rely entirely on Havre till other bases could be developed. All our programmes would vanish at a stroke. I was deeply concerned that this issue should be

calmly probed before it actually came upon us. I therefore
examined it in the following note which I sent to Sir Henry
Wilson and the War Cabinet:

To the War Cabinet.

Very Secret.

A NOTE ON CERTAIN HYPOTHETICAL CONTINGENCIES

April 18, 1918.

1. IF the German offensive continues to prosper, a vital
question will be raised, viz., *whether we should let go our left
hand or our right.* All the movements of stores, munitions,
and depots which are now taking place are affected and ought
to be governed by this decision. It is imperative therefore
to face the situation in advance and have a clear and pro-
foundly considered view.

2. It is possible that we shall not have a free choice. The
course of the German offensive may decide the issue irrespective of our wishes. If they succeeded in an attack along the
coast, which made us let go our left hand from the Channel
ports one after another, we should be forced to pivot by our
right, and would finish up with our left near Abbeville and
our right hand clasping the French. If, on the other hand,
the enemy succeeded in cutting the British Army from the
French by an attack through Amiens towards Abbeville, we
should find ourselves in a Torres Vedras position covering
Calais and Boulogne. Now, which of these two do we dis-
like most? It is very important to decide, because by our
dispositions and exertions we shall be able to influence, and
may be able to determine, how the matter shall be settled.

3. To form a reasonable opinion, the first thing to do is
to look—not at the map of the existing battleground, but at
the map of France as a whole. It then immediately appears
what a very small portion of France is involved in the present
and threatened invasion. It is evident that however important the Channel ports and Flanders may be, they and all
the ground we hold are only a fragment of the country and
nation we are defending, and on whose continued resistance
the future of the land war depends.

4. The next thing is to consider what strategic developments would best suit the enemy. I say '*strategic*' as apart

from the fortune of the battlefield. Of course the break-up of a whole army on the battleground is a short cut to strategic success—is indeed the end at which all strategy aims. But assuming—which is reasonable—there is no such collapse of our army, and that at the worst we make an orderly retirement, presenting a steady front and continuing to fight, what is the best strategy for the Germans to pursue? Which hand would they like us to let go—our right or our left?

5. If the Germans could succeed in sweeping us from the Channel ports and capturing Dunkirk, Calais, and Boulogne, they would gain all those very great advantages which have so often been explained. They can command the Straits of Dover, close the Port of London to all except northabout traffic, render Dover Harbour uncomfortable, bombard a large part of Kent and Sussex, and deprive our armies of their nearest and most convenient bases. But they would remain confronted by the mass of the still unbeaten British and French armies along a line from the neighbourhood of Abbeville so much shortened that, even with greatly reduced forces, it could be solidly held. And behind these armies would be the whole of France open for dilatory retirement or manœuvre. Until those armies were forced to lay down their arms the land war would not be ended. If France wished to make peace, the facilities of retreat open to the British in several directions to the sea or to neutral territory would afford bargaining power to make a military convention providing for the repatriation of that army; and France would be bound to insist on that, even at territorial loss to herself. Therefore, great as are the advantages which Germany would gain by the conquest of the Channel ports, there would be no reason why the war could not be indefinitely prolonged after their loss, provided the French and British armies remained united.

6. If on the other hand the Germans divide the British and French armies from each other at Abbeville, forcing us to let go our right hand and shut ourselves up in a Torres Vedras, they will have the following choice open to them, viz.; whether to wire in and so mask the British and throw their whole force against the French and Paris, or alternatively to hold the French in check while they drive the British into the sea. What would their choice be? What was it at the beginning of the war? Did they not absolutely disdain the Channel ports

while there was a chance of taking Paris and smashing the main army? Had we any difficulty in deciding, when it came to the pinch in those days, whether our—then little—army should cover the Channel ports, or hold on firmly to the French and fight the main battle out in their company?

7. Although the British Army thrown back on the Channel ports might be seriously weakened, yet to drive it into the sea, or to destroy it in its entrenchments, would require an enormous effort. For the Germans to lay siege to such an army, with the almost intact French Army striking at their backs, would seem to be an unwise proceeding. 'Frappez la masse' is a maxim to which the Germans have always given an understanding allegiance. And that would be their shortest road to end the war. It therefore seems probable that they would leave the weakened and exhausted British Army cooped up in its lines around the Channel ports, and try the main conclusion with the French Army. On the morrow of such a victory over the French the British Army would be at their disposal. They could deal with it at their convenience.

All this appears to follow the elementary lines: Divide the enemy's forces into two parts: hold off the weaker part while you beat the stronger: the weaker then is at your mercy.

8. Do not all these considerations go to show that the vital and supreme need is for us to keep connection with the French? Does not experience generally show that armies which get separated from the main army are disposed of at leisure? Is not the sound rule to stand together, retire together, turn together, and strike together, as we did at the Marne? What would have been the position of a British Army which, after Mons, had retreated on the Channel ports, if in its absence the battle of the Marne had been lost by the French? How long would the Belgian Army have held out if they had been cut off in Antwerp? What happened to the Roumanian Army once it was isolated?

9. To sum up: the choice in the hypothetical circumstances now being examined presents itself as follows: (1) To let go the left hand, lose the Channel ports, keep contact with the French, save our army, and continue the land war indefinitely; or (2) to let go the right hand, lose contact with the French, watch them being defeated, then be driven into the sea ourselves, and lose the Channel ports after all.

10. Happily these bleak alternatives are not yet before us, and there are good hopes they will never be. But it is necessary that the question should be promptly examined with the fullest knowledge of the capacities of the various French ports and of the strength of the armies which could be based on each of them.

Wilson replied: 'I agree, as you know, and have asked the Admiralty to get out a paper on their side of the question.'

This issue was put to Foch at the meeting of the Supreme War Council which met at Abbeville on May 1 and 2. Both Wilson and Haig felt that a decision from the Supreme Commander was necessary in order that precautionary preparations could be made. The Chief of the Imperial General Staff persuaded the representatives of the British Government to press insistently for an answer. The utmost that Foch could be induced to admit was that it was more important to retain touch between the two armies than to retain possession of the Channel Ports. But he returned resolutely to his main contention: 'I mean to fight for both. The question, therefore, cannot arise until I am beaten. I will never give up either. 'Ni l'un ni l'autre. Cramponnez partout.' He hazarded a great deal upon the endurance of the British Army. But he was not disappointed.

On the 25th an unlucky event occurred. The French divisions which from the 18th onwards had deployed behind our front, had taken over a portion of the line, which they held in strength with divisional fronts of no more than 3,000 yards. Included in this sector, the French 28th Division held the invaluable height of Scherpenberg and Kemmel, the latter defended by one battalion of the 99th regiment. At dawn the Germans concentrated upon the hill and the trenches round its foot a most astonishing storm of high explosive and gas shells from cannon and *minenwerfer*. It is said that the French masks were only partially proof against the gas. Whatever the cause, the French troops on either side of the hill, after repulsing three infantry attacks, and sustaining heavy losses, gave way and were streaming back by seven o'clock in the morning. Their retirement left the troops on the summit, including some of our own trench-mortar and heavy batteries, to be cut off. A similar fate overwhelmed the British brigade who were holding the trenches on the French left. They were rolled up from the flank, and none escaped death or captivity. The disaster might have taken a still worse turn but for the promptitude with which the Highland Brigade next in succession threw back its right and formed a defensive flank.

There is no doubt that the relations between the French and British commands during the battle period which began on March 21 were not remarkable for a high appreciation of each other's military qualities. The French staff considered that the British had failed and caused a great disaster on the common front, and they openly expressed the opinion that the quality of the British troops at this time was mediocre. The British, on the other hand, felt that the help given under a terrific strain had been both thin and slow, and that the entry of French relieving divisions into the battle was nearly always followed by further retirements. Instances are given by Colonel Boraston of joint attacks which miscarried through the French divisions not being set in motion, although their British comrades were already committed.

He also records a curious incident of which I was myself a witness. At about ten o'clock on April 29 I was breakfasting with Sir Douglas Haig. Sir Herbert Lawrence, his Chief of the Staff, and two or three Aides-de-Camp were present. The Commander-in-Chief had just sat down to his coffee when the following message was put in his hand: 'G.O.C. 39th French Division reports that there is no doubt but that the enemy holds Mont Rouge and Mont Vidaigne. Troops on right of Scherpenberg badly cut up. . . . Enemy reported to be pushing between the Scherpenberg and Mont Rouge.'

Simultaneously there arrived from Plumer a confirmatory message requesting the Chief of the Staff to come at once to the Headquarters of the Second Army. No Reserves of any kind were available and the news if true involved the grim issue discussed in my Memorandum of the 18th. The room was rapidly emptied. Haig disappeared into his office observing, 'The situation is never so bad or so good as first reports indicate': and Lawrence vanished in a motor-car.

I thought I would go and see for myself what was happening, and accordingly I motored to the area of Sir Alexander Godley's Corps, which was the nearest to the reported breakthrough. A violent cannonade loaded the air; but at the Corps Headquarters faces were beaming. The French Commander had telephoned that it was all a mistake and that nothing of importance was occurring. Such accidents from time to time are inevitable. But this is an illustration of the tension under which both the French and British leaders were living in these very hard times.

However, the worst was over for the British Headquarters though they did not know it, and the rest of the war with all its slaughters and exertions contained for them only hopes and triumphs. The capture of Mount Kemmel was the last effort of the Germans in this battle. It is astounding that after having gained so great a prize at so high a cost they did not use it. The decision was Ludendorff's. The war diaries and archives of the German Fourth Army for the period April 9–30, captured by the French, show that so far from urging the Army Staff to press on to victory, it was Ludendorff who suggested that they stand fast and prepare to meet a British counter-stroke. 'In view of the solidarity of the defence,' he wrote, 'it should be considered whether the attack should be interrupted or continued.' To this General von Lossberg, Chief of the Fourth Army Staff, replied that 'our troops encountered everywhere in the field of attack a very solid defence, well distributed in depth and particularly difficult to overcome on account of the numerous machine-gun nests. . . . With the forces at present at our disposal the operation offers no chance of success. Better interrupt it.' And Ludendorff approved. The stubborn defence had succeeded at the moment when it had sustained its most dangerous wound.

So ended the most fierce and intense grapple of the British and Germans. For forty days, from March 21 to the end of April, the main strength of Germany had been ceaselessly devoted to the battery and destruction of the British Army. One hundred and twenty German Divisions had repeatedly assaulted 58 British, piercing the front, gaining great successes and capturing more than a thousand cannon, and seventy or eighty thousand prisoners. During these forty days the British Army had lost in officers 2,161 killed, 8,619 wounded, and 4,023 missing or prisoners: and of other ranks 25,967 killed, 172,719 wounded, and 89,380 missing or prisoners: a total loss of 14,803 officers and 288,066 men.[1] This was more than one-quarter of the whole number of British fighting troops under Sir Douglas Haig's command on March 21. But these terrible losses concentrated in so short a period on a relatively small military organism had not quenched its life-force. No vital position had been wrested from its grip. No despondency had overwhelmed the troops or their leaders. The machine continued to function, and the men continued to fight. Doggedly and dauntlessly they fought without a doubt that whatever their own fate, Britain would come victoriously through as she had always done before. By their stubborn and skilful resistance at every point, by numberless small parties fighting unchronicled till they were blotted out, the British inflicted upon the Germans losses even greater than those they themselves endured, losses irreparable at this period in the war, losses which broke the supreme German effort for victory at the outset, and rang the knell of doom in

[1] *Military Effort*, p. 362.

the ears of the overwrought German people. There fell of the Germans against the British in these same forty days, 3,075 officers killed, 9,305 wounded, and 427 missing or prisoners; and 53,564 other ranks killed, 242,881 wounded and 39,517 missing or prisoners; a total of 12,807 officers and 335,962 men. An advancing army always gathers the prisoners and missing on a scale far exceeding its retreating opponent. These cut off units are the heavy price of retirement, and they are a permanent loss to the defenders. But if—under these reserves—the missing and prisoners are deducted from each side, the fact emerges that the British shot 308,825 Germans during these battles at a cost of 209,466; or briefly three Germans shot for every two British.

It was now to be the turn of our Ally. The flail under which we had suffered was soon to be uplifted against the French. If we had known beforehand what their ordeal was to be, we should have been thankful they had nursed and guarded their remaining strength to face it.

CHAPTER XIX

THE SURPRISE OF THE CHEMIN DES DAMES

Dwindling German Objectives—Foch and Strategic Proportion—Disposition of the Allied Reserve—The Chemin des Dames—The First Warning—Battle of May 27—The American Arrival—Relations between British and French—Paris and its Workshops—Improved Defence system—The Battle of Noyon—Alteration of the Strategic and Numerical Balances—Foch's Personal Position—A General Survey—The Past—The Present—The Future—The Question.

AT the end of April when the battle in the north died down, Ludendorff, finding too many troops in front of him, looked elsewhere. 'The most favourable operation in itself,' he writes,[1] 'was to continue the attack on the English Army at Ypres and Bailleul. . . . Before we could attack here again, the enemy must become weaker and our communications must be improved.' He had thus resigned all the decisive strategic objects for which the German armies had been fighting since March 21. He had first abandoned the great roll-up of the British line from Arras northwards and the general destruction of the British armies, in favour of the more definite but still vital aim of taking Amiens and dividing the British from the French armies. Arrested in this, he had struck in the north to draw British reserves from the Amiens battlefield. But the battle of the Lys, begun as a diversion, had offered the lesser yet still enormous prize of the northern Channel ports. Now he must abandon that; and his strategic ambition, already thrice contracted, must henceforward sink to an altogether lower plane. The fourth

[1] *My War Memories*, p. 615.

German offensive battle of 1918 was to a large extent a mere
bid for a local victory, and apart from its usefulness in divert-
ing Allied troops from the fateful fronts, offered no deadly
strategic possibilities.

Marshal Foch saw with unerring eye the grand and simple
proportion of events. Not deceived by the vast mass of
frightfully important but irrelevant considerations which
obscured the primary issues, he ranged the strategic necessi-
ties of the Allied armies in their true order. Of these the first
beyond compare was the union of the French and British
armies; second, the preservation of the Channel ports; and
third, though in a less decisive sphere, the defence of Paris.
Pétain on the other hand showed on more than one occasion
that his valuations were different. His attitude on the night
of March 24, which precipitated the Doullens Conference,
proves that he would have rated the loss of Paris as a greater
misfortune than the severing of the connection between the
French and British armies. We shall see later a still more
glaring example of this error, which in so accomplished a soldier can only be attributed to the intrusion of sentiment.
Paris could have been occupied by the Germans in June, 1918,
without preventing the collapse of the Central Empires in
November. But the loss of the Channel ports and the consequent halving of the British military effort would have meant
another year of war; and the severance of the British and
French armies might easily have led to their total and final
defeat. Mercifully the good sense of Foch pierced through
the fog of false appearances. From the moment when he
obtained the supreme command, he steadily massed the reserves, in full harmony with the British view, to safeguard the
junction of the British and French armies. And behind him,
with equal comprehension, Clémenceau when the need came
declared: 'I shall fight in front of Paris. I shall fight in Paris.
I shall fight behind Paris.' Thus these great men were able
to exalt their minds above the dearest temptations of their

hearts, and thus we found the path to safety by discerning the beacons of truth.

*   *   *   *   ⸗

It followed from Foch's decision to gather the reserves in Flanders and between Compiègne and Amiens that dangerous denudations must be accepted on other important parts of the front. The movement northwards of so many French divisions was viewed with deep anxiety by Pétain and the French Army Headquarters. Pétain indeed made a strenuous effort to retain the last instalment. But Foch insisted. Thus Ludendorff found, when the battle of the Lys ended in deadlock, that it was not open to him to renew the battle of Amiens. He was already committed to two great bulges which he had conquered at the cost of heavy drafts upon the superior reserves he had gathered for the campaign. In neither could he advance in face of the strength against him, and from both he was unwilling to retire lest he should shatter the glittering but, as he knew well, already brittle confidence of Germany. Each of these bulges had its special disadvantages for the German troops. In the Somme region they were condemned to dwell amid their own devastations, and with communications which, although improved, made the mounting of a first-class offensive impossible. In the Bailleul salient the conditions were far worse. The scale was smaller, but for this very reason the discomfort was more intense. The whole of the conquered ground was commanded by the encircling British artillery. And this artillery, fed with unlimited ammunition and fresh guns, raked and swept the German salient night and day from three quarters of the compass. In this cauldron nearly twenty German divisions must be constantly maintained at a cost which melted the reserves apace.

It must have been with darkening misgivings that Ludendorff selected the point of his next attack. Outwardly all seemed to be going well. Actually all had miscarried. But the consolation of spectacular vengeance yet remained. Immense resources were still in hand. A dazzling victory could yet be won which, though barren in consequences, would still preserve the illusion of increasing success. As early as April 17 the Crown Prince's Army group was ordered urgently to prepare an offensive on the Chemin des Dames, with the object of breaking through between Soissons and Rheims. The arrangements were made with the customary thoroughness and science and with unexampled secrecy. The Seventh and First German Armies assembled twenty-nine divisions for the battle. No less than 1,158 batteries were deployed, and the moment was fixed for 2 a.m. on May 27.

Foch knew as well as Pétain the forfeits to which his wise dispositions exposed the French armies, and both Generals were during the whole of May unable to divine where the blow would fall. Blame has been attributed to the staff of the French Sixth Army. The choleric temperament of its Commander General Duchêne had discouraged and estranged his subordinates, and the machine worked with friction.[1] At this time above all others efforts should have been made, without regard to losses, to pierce the enemy's screen by sudden raids, now here now there, and gain the indispensable information. But nothing of this kind was done successfully either by the Sixth Army or elsewhere along the French front. Four French divisions were in line on the Chemin des Dames, with four more in reserve behind the Aisne. On their right was the Ninth British Army Corps under Sir Alexander Hamilton Gordon, comprising three divisions in the line (the 21st, 8th and 50th), also the 25th division in reserve, all shockingly mutilated in the northern battle, and sent at Foch's earnest desire to what was stated by the French to be the quietest sector of the front in order to refit and train their recruits.

[1] Une humeur de dogue, un grondement perpétuel, un orage de rebuffades, tout de suite les gros mots à la bouche, sans raison.—Pierrefeu, *G.Q.G. Secteur* I, Vol. II, p. 178.

In reply to formal warnings from the British General Headquarters that an attack had been mounted against the Aisne
front, the French Sixth Army Staff stated on the morning of
May 25: 'In our opinion there are no indications that the
enemy has made preparations that would enable him to attack to-morrow.'

What followed is exciting.   At daybreak on the 26th two
German prisoners were taken by the French.   One was a private and the other an *officier-aspirant*, belonging to different
regiments of Jäger.   On the way to Divisional Headquarters
their captors entered into conversation with them.   The
private said there was going to be an attack; the officer con-
tradicted him.   Arrived at the Army Corps Intelligence centre
the prisoners were examined separately.   The officer, ques-
tioned first, was voluble, and declared that the Germans had
no intention of making an offensive on this front.   The in-
terrogation of the private followed.   He said that the soldiers
believed that they would attack that night or the following
night.   He was not sure of the date.   Pressed, he said that
cartridges and grenades had already been distributed, but
not the field rations.   He had seen the previous day near his
billets soldiers belonging to Guards regiments.   He knew no
more.   The officer was then recalled.   He was told that the
laws of war had in no way forced him to speak, but that he
had volunteered statements for which he would be held responsible.   To give false information was the act of a spy.
On this he became visibly perturbed, and under pressure gave
in the end the most complete details of the attack which im-
pended the next day.   It was already three o'clock in the afternoon of the 26th.   The alarm was given, and the troops available took up their battle positions.

Pierrefeu has described the terrible hours which Pétain and
the French Headquarters Staff now endured far away at
Provins.[1]   They knew that an immense disaster was certain.

[1] G.Q.G. Section I, Vol. II., p. 187.

They knew that no reinforcements could reach the scene for several days, and thereafter for a still longer period only at the rate of two divisions a day. Meanwhile there was nothing in human power that could be done. All through the night they sat in their silent offices, bowed under the blow about to fall and suffering another form of the tortures to which the troops were doomed. At one o'clock next morning the German barrage descended on a thirty-kilometre front, and three hours later eighteen divisions advanced upon the four French and three refitting British divisions. Although the troops on the ground were alert, the strategic surprise was complete and overwhelming.

'After three-and-a-half hours' artillery and trench-mortar preparation,' says the Crown Prince,[1] 'the divisions surged forward against the Chemin des Dames. . . . The small enemy force holding the position, six French and three English trench divisions, were overrun and the Chemin des Dames and the Aisne-Marne Canal reached in one swoop. As early as the afternoon our leading units were over the Aisne. By the evening the centre of the Third Army had already reached the Vesle on both sides of Fismes. A break-through with a depth of twenty kilometres had been attained in one day. The Aisne-Marne Canal was also crossed by the left wing of the Seventh Army.'

A most stubborn defence was made by the three British divisions which were in the line, and by the 25th Division almost immediately involved. On their right stood the 45th French-Algerian Division which, not being itself attacked, gave energetic assistance. Hinging on this, the British line swung back under immense pressure on its front and with its left continually compromised. The retiring British found behind them fortunately the hilly and wooded country to the west of Rheims, which helped the defence in a receding battle. The 19th British Division had also luckily arrived at Chalons

[1] *My War Experiences*, p. 318.

for rest and recuperation, and on the fourth day they sustained the British line. The 21st Division was by then practically destroyed, and by June 1 the whole five British divisions were hardly equal to the full strength of one. All the troops bore themselves as on the Lys a month earlier. Battalions were completely exterminated, and a large portion of the artillery perished with their guns upon the field. The

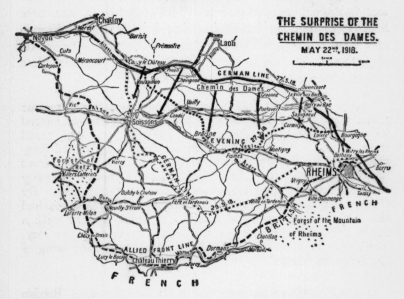

THE SURPRISE OF THE
CHEMIN DES DAMES.
MAY 22ᴺᴰ. 1918.

French villagers in their ignorance and terror assailed the retreating troops with hostile demonstrations.

Meanwhile upon the British left the German punch had smashed right through. General Duchene's staff delayed too long the destruction of the bridges across the Aisne, and most of them fell intact into the hands of the invaders. By June 2 Soissons had fallen and the Germans had reached the Marne at Château-Thierry.

Pierrefeu has described in a moving passage the next event. Now suddenly the roads between Provins and the front

towards Meaux and towards Coulommiers began to be filled
with endless streams of Americans. The impression made
upon the hard-pressed French by this seemingly inexhaustible
flood of gleaming youth in its first maturity of health and vigour was prodigious. None were under twenty, and few were
over thirty. As crammed in their lorries they clattered along
the roads, singing the songs of a new world at the tops of their
voices, burning to reach the bloody field, the French Headquarters were thrilled with the impulse of new life. 'All felt,'
he says, 'that they were present at the magical operation of
the transfusion of blood. Life arrived in floods to reanimate
the mangled body of a France bled white by the innumerable
wounds of four years.' Indeed the reflection conformed with
singular exactness to the fact. Half trained, half organised,
with only their courage, their numbers and their magnificent
youth behind their weapons, they were to buy their experience at a bitter price. But this they were quite ready to do.

*   *   *   *   *

The misfortunes of the Battle of the Chemin des Dames
had the remarkable effect of improving the relations between
the British and French armies. After a surprise so glaring
and a retreat of twenty kilometres in a single day—the record
for all battles on the Western Front—the French were in no
position to maintain the airs of superiority which they had
been unable to conceal from the Italians after Caporetto or
altogether from the British after the 21st of March. Up till
the moment when they in their turn felt the force of a Ludendorff offensive, they had complacently assumed that the
French Army contained the only troops who could really
hold a front under modern conditions. These illusions had
been swept away by the German scythe. The intensity of
their common tribulations united the Allies more closely than
ever. Moreover, the French command were deeply grieved
at the destructive losses suffered by the five British divisions

committed to their care for a period of recuperation. They paid their tribute in generous and soldierly terms to the fighting achievements of these troops. The words of General Maistre, the Commander of the Group of Armies concerned, may be here transcribed: 'With a doggedness, permit me to say thoroughly English, submerged by the hostile flood, you have reconstituted without failing new units to carry on the struggle which have at last enabled us to form the dyke by which this deluge has been mastered. That achievement no Frenchman who was a witness will forget.' [1] The 2nd Devons and the 5th Battery of the Forty-fifth British Field Artillery Brigade were awarded the Croix de Guerre in consequence of their having fought until only the memory remained.

* * * * *

The advance of the Germans to Château-Thierry, barely a hundred kilometres from Paris, confronted me with problems almost as serious and quite as imminent as those which had glared at us during the Battle of the Lys. I was responsible among other things for the whole supply of aeroplanes and aviation material of all kinds. The Ministry of Munitions was a gigantic shop from which the Air Ministry ordered all they wanted. Under the incredible activities of Sir William Weir, then Secretary of State, the Air Force demands became staggering. We discovered that the French had a large surplus manufacturing capacity. I had therefore, in agreement with Loucheur, directed Sir Arthur Duckham to place enormous orders with them. The French factories on which we depended for an essential part of our programme were mostly grouped around Paris. The danger to the capital required elaborate plans for moving these establishments southwards in case of need, and at the same time a very nice decision whether and when to put them into operation. If we moved without cause, we interrupted production. If we tarried too

[1] *Sir Douglas Haig's Command*, Vol. II.

long, we should not be able to get our machinery away. Paris was calm and even pleasant in these days of uncertainty. The long-range German cannon, which threw its shells about every half-hour, had effectually cleared away nearly all those who were not too busy nor too poor. The city was empty and agreeable by day, while by night there was nearly always the diversion of an air raid. The spirit of Clémenceau reigned throughout the capital. 'We are now giving ground, but we shall never surrender. We shall be victorious if the Public Authorities are equal to their task.'

Ludendorff had now made a third bulge in the Allied front. In all three the German troops were uncomfortable, their communications extremely inferior, and their general strategic position delicate. It seemed probable that they would try to bite off or beat in the French salient which jutted out between Montdidier and Château-Thierry as far as Noyon. The deep forest region about Villers-Cotterets and the fact that there was only a single line of railway for all the Germans in the Château-Thierry bulge, made an attack from an eastern direction unlikely. The front before Compiègne from Montdidier to Noyon was clearly the most interesting. M. Clémenceau had authorised and even urged me to go everywhere, see everything, and 'tell Lloyd George what we are doing.' Accordingly as the work of the Inter-Allied Munitions Conference which was then proceeding permitted, I visited the armies of Generals Humbert and Debeny, who awaited the expected shock. I knew both these Generals personally, and was still better acquainted with General Fayolle who commanded the Army Group. One could reach the front line from Paris in less than three hours, and I followed with the closest attention the improved methods of defence which the French were adopting. Nothing of consequence was now offered to the German opening bombardment. A strong picquet line of detached machine-gun nests, carefully concealed, was alone in contact with the enemy.

Behind these devoted troops, for whom an assault could only
mean destruction, was a zone three or four thousand yards
deep, in which only strong points were held by comparatively
small forces.   It was not until at least 7,000 yards separated
them from the hostile batteries that the real resistance of the
French Infantry and Artillery was prepared.   When one saw
all the fortifications and devices, the masses of batteries and

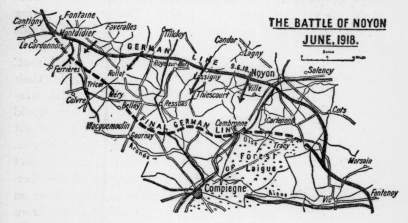

machine guns, with which the main line of defence bristled,
and knew that this could not be subjected to heavy bombardment until the stubborn picquets far in front had been exterminated, it seemed difficult to believe that any troops in the
world could carry the whole position from front to rear in a
single day.

On the evening of June 8 I walked over the centre of the
French line in front of Compiègne.   The presage of battle
was in the air.   All the warnings had been given, and every
one was at his post.   The day had been quiet, and the sweet-
ness of the summer evening was undisturbed even by a cannon shot.   Very calm and gallant, and even gay, were the
French soldiers who awaited the new stroke of fate.   By the
next evening all the ground over which they had led me was

in German hands, and most of those with whom I had talked
were dead or prisoners.

Early on the morning of the 9th the Eighteenth German
Army began what they have called the Battle of Noyon, and
at the same time the Seventh German Army attacked south-
west of Soissons. The whole of the threatened front was thus
on fire. The severity of this onslaught lasted for two days
only. The Germans penetrated to a depth of fifteen kilometres, and set their feet on the heights before Compiègne.
But the methods of defence exacted a heavy toll, and a wise
elasticity in the use of ground enabled the French to economise losses.   From the 11th onwards Fayolle began to launch
carefully prepared counter-attacks in great force, particularly
in the direction of Méry. These continued throughout the
12th and 13th; but already on the 11th Ludendorff had felt
the task beyond his power. 'In consequence,' he says,[1] 'of
the great accumulation of enemy troops G.H.Q. directed the
Eighteenth Army to break off the attack on the 11th, in order
to avoid casualties. It was quite evident that the attack
commenced in the meantime by the Seventh Army south-
west of Soissons would not get through. The action of the
Eighteenth Army had not altered the strategical situation
. . . nor had it provided any fresh tactical data.'

So far in all this year the Allies had experienced nothing
but recoil. The martial might of Germany lay heavy on all.
The sense of grappling with a monster of seemingly unfathom-
able resources and tireless strength, invulnerable—since
slaughter even on the greatest scale was no deterrent—could
not be excluded from the mind. No one hoped for a swift
result. But the idea that the war could reach any end other
than the total defeat of Germany was strictly excluded even
from private conversation. All the dominant personalities
were resolved to fight on to victory, and the soldiers with simple faith took this for granted. Says Ludendorff:[2] 'It was

[1] *My War Memories*, p. 634.   [2] *Ibid.*, p. 642.

certainly discouraging that our two great attacks had not forced a decision. That they had been victories was obvious. . . . The evil effect of disillusionment was doubled by the fact that we could not overcome it in our then state of mind.' But they were not victories: they were only placards. Of the five great battles which had been fought, the first three against the British had failed to achieve any one of the progressively diminishing strategic results at which they had aimed. The fourth against the French was a local victory, very spectacular but without strategic consequence; and the last, the Battle of Noyon, was a very decided arrest. The Supreme offensive was in slack water. The 11th of June on the French front had marked just such a mile-stone in the war as had the 12th of April with the British Army. On the German side, in spite of sensational triumphs, all was 'disillusionment.' Behind the Allied front, with all their bitter experiences, the foundation of confidence was solid.

These three months of ceaseless battle had indeed witnessed a profound alteration of the strategic balance. The main forces of Germany were now deeply committed. The sovereign element of surprise without which no great offensive was possible, depended upon the power to have simultaneously in readiness on different parts of the front four or five attacks of the first magnitude. This had been the baffling factor to the Allies before the 21st of March. But most of these had now already been let off. The remaining possibilities open to Ludendorff were restricted and to a large extent defined. His reservoirs were low; ours were filling full.

The balance of numbers had turned heavily. The British had actually killed and wounded or captured nearly four hundred thousand Germans in the five weeks' grapple, while all their own losses in men and material had by the activities of their Government been more than replaced. Indeed our Army at the end of June was somewhat stronger than on the eve of the 21st of March. Divisions had been drawn from

Italy, from Salonica and from Egypt. Masses of troops had been released from home by the War Office rising superior at long last to the absurd fear of invasion. Sedentary divisions of older men had been formed to hold the trench lines. When the time came they proved they could march as well as stand. Sir Douglas Haig was conscious of a continued accretion of strength; and as the event was to prove, he was able to measure it better than any one else.

The resources of France, so prodigally spent at the beginning, so jealously husbanded in the later years, were sufficient for a final effort. And behind them the Americans gathered in tens of thousands day by day. By this date the British Marine alone, military and merchant, had carried and convoyed to France, without the loss of a life from enemy action, nearly three quarters of a million American troops. All these facts justified confidence in the successful termination of the year's campaign, and that the next year would be decisive.

The personal position of Marshal Foch after the 27th of May was not however entirely unshaken. On him France fixed the prime responsibility of having diverted the French reserves to cover the juncture of the British and French armies. The appointment of a Generalissimo had only been carried in the face of serious and natural oppositions. The firstfruits of 'unity of command' and of Foch's personal direction of the front had been a blazing disaster. Strong undercurrents ran of complaint and reproach. The British did not think they had been well treated in their intense trial. Moreover, there were reasonable grounds for misgiving. Unlike Haig or Pétain, Marshal Foch had not at his disposal the great machinery of a General Staff. He acted only through what he has pleasingly described as 'ma famille militaire,'— a small band of devoted officers who had throughout the war shared his varied fortunes. At their head stood a certain young General Weygand, alert, discreet and silent in manner, afterwards to become better known. Whether this extremely

restricted circle would be able to inform their Chief upon the
vast and innumerable masses of technical detail which must
be mastered before the operations of great modern armies can
be weighed and selected from among alternatives, was a
question at that time without an answer. On this account
also many doubts were entertained. Nevertheless Marshal
Foch, building his house on the rock of strategic truth, possessed his soul in patience.

*   *   *   *   *

During this period of hard tension the Imperial War Cabinet comprising the Prime Ministers of the Dominions was
frequently in Session in London. Sir Henry Wilson one day
in presenting to them an appreciation of the whole position
went back to the beginning, and took occasion to refer to
my work with him in the years before the war. This led me
to prepare for the Dominion Ministers a short general survey of past, present and future as I saw them then. I print
it as I wrote it. It is a record of that darkest hour which we
are told precedes the dawn.

A Note on the War.

To the Imperial War Cabinet.

June 22, 1918.

1. Before the war the British military authorities fore-
casted with accuracy what the German plan of campaign
would be, and Sir Henry Wilson, in particular, as early as
August, 1911, unfolded to the Committee of Imperial Defence
a completely true picture of the German attack in the West,
through Belgium towards Paris, and also of the Russian
weakness and tardy mobilisation in the East. On the other
hand, our military advisers took a far too sanguine view of
the relative strength and efficiency of the French and German
armies. On the outbreak of war, the overpowering need was
to stem the German rush, first on Paris, and secondly on the
Channel Ports, and no one could think of anything else on
land till this was done. By the end of November, as the

Chief of the Staff has explained, Paris and the Channel Ports were saved, and the German onslaught brought to a standstill. The first phase of the war, which may be called "stemming the rush," thus came to an end.

2. The second phase covered a period of 18 to 20 months, viz., from the end of 1914 to the Battle of the Somme in July, 1916. During the whole of this period the position in the West was that the Anglo-French armies were strong enough to hold the Germans, but not strong enough to attack them with any chance of piercing their fortified lines. The main theatre, *i.e.* the theatre where the main forces are gathered, ceased to be for the time being the decisive theatre, *i.e.* the theatre where an important decision can be obtained. These conditions were clearly recognised in the British Cabinet. They were disputed by both the British and French military authorities. The divergence of view arising from different estimates of forces and values led to the loss of opportunities which will never recur.

3. The politicians were in the main generally convinced that the deadlock in the West would continue until a great British Army could be called into being, and equipped with a powerful artillery and plentiful munitions. They therefore immediately looked for other theatres in which our forces could gain decisive results in the interval. Two great operations, each involving the concerted action of our naval, military and diplomatic resources, presented themselves: first, the rallying of the group of small States at the north-western corner of Europe, thus turning the enemy's right flank, obtaining command of the Baltic, and forming contact with Russia in the north; or secondly, rallying the group of small States at the south-eastern corner of Europe, striking down Turkey before Germany could organise her, and establishing contact with Russia from the south. Of these two policies, the first was clearly the more difficult, and was never perhaps possible, having regard to our resources. The second however was not only possible but easy of accomplishment if the proper measures had been taken. Turkey was isolated from Germany by the Balkan States. She was ill-organised and ill-prepared. She was menaced by Russia. We held better cards than the Germans in regard to every single one of the Balkan States. The partition of the Turkish Empire offered the means of

satisfying every appetite. Lastly, the naval situation was entirely favourable. Our margins in the North Sea had been greatly increased since the declaration of war. The German submarines had not become formidable, and the destruction of Von Spee had completed the clearance of the German warships from the surface of the oceans. An amphibious operation to strike down Turkey before she could raise her head, and to unite the Balkan States against their natural foes, the Turkish and Austrian Empires, was well within the scope of the naval and military resources at our disposal, after providing an ample superiority over the Germans in the North Sea and sufficient forces to defend actively the front in France and Flanders. It was therefore towards the southern flank of the enemy's line, to Turkey and to the Balkans, that our operations were directed—but alas half-heartedly.

4. The natural tendency of the naval and military point of view is to confuse the main and the decisive theatres. Wherever the main part of the Army or the main part of the fleet is assembled, always claims their partisanship.[1] Accordingly, the professional opinion of the navy grudged and resisted the employment at the Dardanelles of every unit, even the most worthless; and the professional opinion of the Army delayed, grudged, and stinted the employment of every soldier and of every shell required for the Eastern campaign. These tendencies, which would have been overborne by success, became at the first check overpowering. The Eastern enterprise was therefore cast away, with consequences of measureless disaster.

Bulgaria, always the key of the Balkans, remained undecided while the fate of the Dardanelles hung in the balance. Her course was determined by the loss of the Battle of Suvla Bay. The destruction of Serbia followed immediately, and the destruction of Roumania a year later. Turkey was gripped and organised by the Germans, entailing great diversions of our forces to Egypt and Mesopotamia. Adding the loss involved by these diversions to the loss arising from the destruction of Serbia and Roumania, the paralysis of Greece, and the hostility of Bulgaria, our failure to prosecute the Eastern enterprise successfully may well have equalled the addition of two million soldiers to the ranks of our enemies.

[1] I have not corrected this war-time grammar, as the sense is clear.

Besides this we lost the means to succour and animate Russia by direct contact.

5. The third phase of the war supervenes upon the second. After the year 1915, there were no hopes of gaining any good results in Turkey or the Balkans. The Germans were everywhere in complete communication and control. In consequence, Allied Armies large enough to achieve success in those theatres were too large for the carrying capacity of our seaborne tonnage. Moreover, the submarine had become formidable in the Mediterranean, and the military weakness of Russia was plainly apparent. Half the soldiers lost and half the shells fired in Artois in May, and at Loos and in Champagne in September, 1915, resolutely used, would have achieved for us the whole south-eastern theatre of war in that year; but in 1916 four times their number could not have retrieved the position. The extinction of other possibilities left France therefore the only theatre open to us.[1]

Meanwhile however a great British Army had come into being, abundantly supplied with munitions. The third or as it may be called "The Slogging Phase" then began. This lasted from the beginning of the Battle of the Somme, the 1st July, 1916, to the end of the Paschendale attacks in November, 1917. During the whole of this period the British armies, sometimes alone and sometimes assisted by the French, were hurled almost continuously, or with the briefest intervals for recovery, in assaults upon the fortified German lines. I have personally always held the view that at no time in this period were we strong enough, in the absence of some entirely novel method of attack applied on a gigantic scale, e. g., tanks or gas, to break through the skilful German defence, reinforced as it always was, and still is, by the power of giving ground wherever necessary without serious consequence. Still, such was the heroic gallantry of the armies and the determination of their leaders, so powerful was the artillery of which they disposed, that the hope of victory and the sense of mastery were never quenched in the hearts of our troops until the mud deluge of Paschendale.

The most hopeful climax of these operations was however

[1] I did not think it useful to discuss in this paper a surprise attack in 1916 by all the forces in the Mediterranean theatre upon the Gallipoli peninsula. No one would have weighed it seriously at this time.

probably reached at the end of the year 1916 in the later phases of the Battle of the Somme. At this time the enemy were at their greatest strain. They were weakened by their folly at Verdun. They were attacked simultaneously by the British and French armies astride of the Somme. Brusiloff gained his great victories on the Austrian front, and Roumania plunged into the war. The exertions which the Germans made in this emergency should make us realise the strength of our foe. By dint of them they managed to reach the winter, striking down Roumania meanwhile.

6. The Germans did not feel themselves strong enough in the spring of 1917 to withstand the renewed onslaught of the British and French armies. They therefore ruptured the Anglo-French plans for combined action by suddenly withdrawing their line from the Somme battlefields almost to St. Quentin and Cambrai. They thus placed a broad belt of devastated country between them and their would-be assailants, and also between the British and French armies. By this manœuvre they avoided the kind of long-prepared accumulated blow they have struck at us this year, and only had to face through the rest of 1917 disconnected attacks by the British, and occasionally by the French. The campaign of 1917 therefore became very disastrous to us. Although each military episode, taken by itself, wore the aspect of a fine success, with captures of ground and guns and prisoners, in reality we were consuming our strength without any adequate result.

7. Late in the year a false naval argument played its part in swaying military policy. The harbours of Zeebrugge and Ostend were represented as being the source of the submarine warfare, and their capture or suppression was alleged to be vital. As a matter of fact, these harbours of course have never been and could never be the main base of submarine warfare. That has only been directed and can only be directed from the permanent naval bases of Germany in the estuaries of the Elbe, the Weser, and the Ems. Ostend and Zeebrugge were serious annoyances, but as objectives they were utterly inadequate to the sacrifices demanded of the Army in order to secure the Flanders Coast. Moreover, the season of the year was advanced. The Russian collapse had taken place; nobody else was fighting; the numbers of the enemy on the front attacked were almost equal to our own; the

direction of the attack was perceived and thoroughly prepared against by elaborate semi-permanent fortifications. In these circumstances the amazing efforts of the British armies could have no other result than to weaken themselves.

The incidental disaster which happened to Italy was not so harmful as it looked. Her renewed effort more than made up for the heavy losses sustained.

8. While our commanders were intent upon the battle and in hopes of gaining successes in the nick of time, they do not seem to have realised the awful consequences of the collapse of Russia. But in November and December this apprehension grew with politicians and generals, both British and French. The flow of German divisions and batteries from Russia to the West was unceasing for many months until finally a power had been accumulated which, after marking down every division of which we could dispose, left the enemy with a punching force of nearly fifty divisions. The enemy's military methods differ from our own. In attack the German uses Surprise, in defence he uses Concrete. Our defensive problem this year is far more difficult than that which the Germans solved successfully in 1917. On every occasion in 1917 (except at Cambrai) the Germans knew where the attack would fall. Every attack (except Cambrai) was indicated by several days' bombardment, apart from every evidence of ill-camouflaged preparation. Every German position was defended by lines of solid shell-proof structures sheltering machine guns, and ample reserves were held in rear to arrest a successful advance beyond the limits of our offensive barrage. Lastly, the Germans could always afford to give up some of the territory they overran so easily at the beginning of the war.

Our position this year has been very different. The initiative has passed completely to the enemy. His attack is mounted actually or in dummy over practically the whole battle-front, and besides we can never exclude his irruption at some quite unexpected point. We, on the other hand, have at least four places—Calais, Amiens, Paris, Verdun—which we regard as capital. The enemy can therefore ring the changes on a succession of vital points, before each one of which we have little or no ground to spare. Meanwhile the use of gas and smoke has given new facilities to the offensive,

and our methods of fortifications are still primitive compared
with those of the Germans.

In this dire situation nothing has saved us except the stam-
ina of our armies and the physical difficulties of persevering
in an offensive after a certain distance. The stubborn resistance which the enemy has encountered, the bloody repulses
which in spite of his successes he has sustained on the greatest
scale, and the resources in men and material which the threat
of utter ruin has extorted from the Allies, have gone far to
equalise the struggle. It is even probable that we shall end
this campaign of agony and disaster in far better posture than
we began it. But what are we going to do then?

9. This is the question to which I have been leading up.
If I have tried to pick out as I see them the salient points in
the past, it is with the object of showing that there are now
and in the immediate future just as vital decisions to be taken
if we can only secure the necessary vision and command. It
may be that the Imperial War Cabinet will be able to impart
to the Allied conduct of the war that general design and true
selection of vital objectives which we have never yet been
able to obtain.

10. There are two perfectly simple things to do. They
have long been staring us in the face. Everybody sees them,
but they see so much else at the same time that nothing effective has yet been done: (1) Above all things reconstitute the
fighting front in the East; (2) make a plan for an offensive
battle in France in 1919, choosing the period of climax and
subordinating, as far as pressure of circumstances will allow,
every intervening event to that supreme purpose.

If we cannot reconstitute the fighting front against Germany
in the East, no end can be discerned to the war. Vain will
be all the sacrifices of the peoples and the armies. They will
only tend to prolong the conflict into depths which cannot be
plumbed. We must not take 'No' for an answer either from
America or from Japan. We must compel events instead of
acquiescing in their drift. Surely now when Czech divisions
are in possession of large sections of the Siberian Railway and
in danger of being done to death by the treacherous Bolsheviks, some effort to rescue them can be made?[1] Every man

[1] Some of the Bohemian prisoners taken by Brusiloff in 1916 had
been formed into a Czech Army Corps which fought with resolution

should ask himself each day whether he is not too readily
accepting negative solutions. May we not assume that
President Wilson will regard the rescue of the Czechs as an
obligation of honour? Who can rescue them except the
Japanese? . . .

11. Secondly, we must organise the offensive battle for
1919. It will be no use thinking about this in the winter
when we may hope our present anxieties will be at an end.
It will be too late then. Unless while we are fighting for our
lives all this summer we can look ahead and plan for 1919,
we shall be in the same melancholy position next year as we
are this. In this war the initiative can only be seized as the
result of plans made nearly a year ahead and through the
successful overcoming of some great difficulty. Is it not possible at the present time to conceive and visualise a victorious
offensive battle in the summer of 1919, to manufacture all
the apparatus necessary to that battle, and to subordinate
intervening arrangements, as far as daily needs will let us, to
bringing about a situation favourable to that battle? Do the
means of beating the German armies in the West in 1919
exist? Can the men be procured? If so the mechanisms can
be prepared. We still have the time. Have we the will-
power and the command?

against the Austrian Empire. The Russian revolution and the Bol-
shevik desertion of the Allied cause left these soldiers in a forlorn
position, from which their discipline and firm political convictions
ultimately extricated them.

CHAPTER XX

THE UNFOUGHT CAMPAIGN

'The God of the Bees is the future.'
[*Maeterlinck.*]

Two Practical Steps to Finality—Need of American Troops—General Pershing's Fine Decision—My Mission to Clémenceau—President Wilson's Valiant Response—An Act of Fate—Equipment of the American Armies—Mr. Stettinius—Mr. Baruch—Nitrates and Diplomacy—The American Artillery Problem—Its Solution—Cordial Co-operation—A 'gentleman's' agreement—Munition Workers' Unrest—The Coventry Strike—Château Verchocq—The Mechanical Battle—My Letter to General Harington—The Man-Power Problem 1918 and 1919—July and August Memoranda—The 10,000 Caterpillars—Foch's Endorsement—Future Hopes.

DURING these tremendous struggles, while the fate of the Channel ports and even of the union between the British and French armies hung in the balance, by far the greater part of my duties and thoughts lay in the future. Throughout the summer the Munitions Council worked for a campaign which, in God's mercy, was never fought. To make sure of victory in 1919 was an aim at once possible and imperative. Dominated by this conviction, I concentrated all time and thought that could be spared from day-to-day emergencies upon the task. I had neither the responsibility nor the power; but with such influence as I possessed I tried to turn British and Allied policy to two great practical steps: first to bring American manhood into Europe on the largest scale as fast as possible; secondly to devise the plan and prepare the apparatus of a mechanical battle of decisive magnitude. In this chapter, between the stemming of the German onslaught and the beginning of the brilliant period which all unknown was now approaching, I shall endeavour to give the reader some account of both these measures.

I had long been disappointed at the slow rate at which American troops were being transported across the Atlantic.[1] I did not believe that the resources either of the Admiralty or of the British Mercantile Marine were being used to the full. I always held that first importance should be assigned to the transportation of American soldiers, and that all the formidable difficulties of their training, equipment and supply could be surmounted later in their turn. A week before Ludendorff struck his first blow I had minuted to the War Cabinet as follows:—

AMERICA AND SHIPPING

March 14, 1918.

I trust that the War Cabinet will not allow themselves to be deflected by the serious difficulties which no doubt exist from their resolve to transport the additional American divisions in British ships to Europe. The infantry of the British Army has been reduced by 25%, or approximately 170 battalions. The addition of 72 American battalions will still leave that Army substantially smaller than it was last year, and therefore well within the compass of our cross-channel transportation and railway system on the British Front.

The immense political and military advantages of drawing American manhood into the war, and of thus partially filling the gap caused by the diminution of our own forces, ought to outweigh all other considerations and make us ready to submit to the further reduction in food, civil imports and munitions rather than lose the benefit which should now be reached. It is emphatically a case where the difficulties ought to be surmounted and mastered, and not recoiled from as soon as they present themselves. A true sense of relative values at the present time would assign supreme priority to the rapid augmentation by every conceivable means of the numbers of American soldiers in France.

[1] See page 3 of Memorandum of Oct. 21, 1917.

Quite apart from the imperious military need, the intermingling of British and American units on the field of battle and their endurance of losses and suffering together may exert an immeasurable effect upon the future destiny of the English-speaking people, and will afford us perhaps the only guarantee of safety if Germany emerges stronger from the War than she entered it.

The Prime Minister had from the beginning formed these general views independently. He used all his powers at every stage to give effect to them. He had already arranged for 72 American battalions to be attached in the first instance to British Units. The intense peril in which we seemed to stand after the Twenty-first of March spurred him to renewed exertions, and at the same time rendered those exertions fruitful. Confronted with the extreme crisis, General Pershing and General Bliss presented themselves to General Foch on March 28 and spontaneously, in the finest manner, placed the whole of their resources in France for the time being at his disposal. Their plans for the development of the great American Army would be subordinated to the emergency wherever necessary. The American divisions, or battalions if need be, would enter the line forthwith in spite of their training and organisation being incomplete. This decision was at the true height of circumstances, and in itself went far to repair the injuries of Ludendorff's inroad.

As soon as I was able to report that all measures to make good the losses of material had been taken and would be immediately effective, the Prime Minister sent me again to France upon a somewhat delicate mission. On the morning of March 28 I started for Paris with instructions to see Clémenceau and if possible Foch, and find out whether the French were willing to make a vigorous attack on the Southern flank of the battlefields to take some of the pressure off our armies. Such a direct but irregular inquiry might well have encountered a rebuff. Arrived in Paris, I therefore asked our Liaison Officer, General Sackville-West, to explain matters to Clémenceau. But the Tiger brushed all formalities aside. We would start together for the front, he said, at 8 o'clock the next morning. We would visit Foch at Beauvais, Rawlinson at Dury, and all the French Headquarters within reach. We would learn for ourselves on the spot and through all the responsible persons exactly what the effort of the French Army would be.

We spent the whole of the 30th at the front, saw all the commanders, got sufficiently near the shells to satisfy the President of the Council, dined with Pétain in his Headquarters train, and returned to Paris after midnight. Tired out, I was about to go to bed when a long cipher telegram from the Prime Minister arrived. Mr. Lloyd George repeated the message he had that day sent to President Wilson appealing for the despatch of American troops on the largest possible scale, whether formed in divisions or in the smallest formations, or even as drafts to British units. He directed me to see Clémenceau at once and to urge him in a separate telegram to support this appeal in the strongest manner. The Tiger received me at 9 a. m., quite unaffected by the fatigue of the previous day, and wrote while I waited a most vigorous and moving appeal. The action which President Wilson took in response to these requests was courageous in the last degree. Henceforward the main effort of the United States was to send men to France up to the fullest limit of ocean transport. In large formations or in small, trained or half-trained, without regard to armament, equipment or supplies, American manhood was to proceed to the war. The use to be made of all these great numbers of men, their organisation, their training, their ammunition, their food and clothing —all were questions to be solved later on. This was an act of faith of the highest merit. No one who did not possess that intense form of power which comes from expressing the will of a free people could have dared to decree a policy in appearance so improvident and even reckless. A hundred valid arguments existed against it, but all were relegated to a lower plane. From this moment the United States poured men into France, and by this action more than any other which it was in their power to take helped to bring the war to a speedy termination.

To fight in defence of his native land is the first duty of the citizen. But to fight in defence of some one else's native land is a different proposition. It may also be a sacred obligation, but it involves a higher conception. Willingly to cross the ocean and fight for strangers, far from home, upon an issue in the making of which one has had no say, requires a wide outlook upon human affairs and a sense of world responsibility. Canada, Australia, New Zealand, drawn by common citizenship under the Crown, had from the outset revealed this noble power of comprehension, and had made their decision good across broader spaces on the battlefields of three years. They had endured slaughters which no American army was destined to know, and their achievements are upon record. But the decision which in the emergency President Wilson took to remedy the consequences of previous long delay involved personal deprivations of a peculiar kind for the soldiers of the United States. To serve in one's national army, under one's own leader, amid a great mass of men animated by a common spirit is one ordeal. To serve in isolated divisions or brigades or even regiments under the orders of foreign Generals, flanked on either side by troops of different race and language and of unknown comradeship or quality, is another. Amid the hardships and terrors of war the soldier is accustomed to find his last remaining comfort of mind in being with his own friends and fellow-countrymen, sustained by the esprit de corps at least of 'The Battalion.' But in the dire need of the great struggle and in a loyal desire to share the tribulations of their allies, American soldiers by scores of thousands readily obeyed orders from their Government to serve, albeit under the general supervision of Pershing, as isolated companies or even platoons in British or French units in order that the largest number might come under the fire of the enemy at an earlier period.

Such conduct required from the Allies the utmost loyal exertions to equip the forces so trustfully sent. At this I laboured incessantly. My duties brought me into intimate and constant contact with the leading representatives in Europe of the United States Supply Services, as well as with General Bliss and upon occasion with General Pershing. From the first we worked together without a single misunderstanding or disagreement. No Government could have found a more able servant than Mr. Stettinius, the representative of the American War Department. To business aptitudes of the highest order, he added a delightful simplicity and directness of character. He was already experienced in the munitions sphere, having handled the bulk of the great affairs which the British Government transacted through Messrs. Morgan before the American declaration of war. This event changed fundamentally our arrangements for buying American supplies. Morgans' ceased to be our agents, and in August, 1917, an agreement was signed under which all our requirements from the United States were to be undertaken by an official Purchasing Commission. This consisted of three members of the War Industries Board, Mr. Bernard M. Baruch, Mr. Robert S. Lovett and Mr. Robert S. Bookings. The War Industries Board, of which Mr. Baruch was Chairman, had exceptional powers as a final executive authority in the determination of priority between competing military and other claims, in the allocation of materials and manufacturing resources, and also in the fixing of prices and the control of capital issues. Sir Charles Gordon and Mr. Brand acted in Washington as my principal representatives in dealing with this body.

The arrangements worked excellently. We 'carried on the

war in common' in every sense of the expression. We transferred masses of every kind of material, in every stage of production, from one ledger to the other in accordance with our
very different needs as easily as two friends might share a
luncheon-basket. There was no rigmarole or formalism in our
affairs. We ransacked our cupboards to find anything the
American troops in France required, and the Americans on
the other hand, once the case was clearly explained in conversation, drew without hesitation from their own remoter
programmes for our more urgent needs. We built common
factories for tanks and aviation material. The Americans offered us their earliest supply of mustard gas. At the end I
accepted from Mr. Stettinius a contract of over £100,000,000
sterling to supply the whole requirements of the United States
Army in medium artillery (6-in. guns and howitzers) for the
campaign of 1919. The principles of this contract were simple. We guaranteed the United States we would make no
profit, and they guaranteed us we should suffer no loss, however the event might turn.

It was not until after the war was over that I had the
pleasure of meeting Mr. Baruch, the Chairman of the War Industries Board; but almost daily telegrams soon put us on
excellent terms. I could feel at the other end of the cable
a strong clear mind taking quick decisions and standing by
them. After a few months' co-operation he paid me the
very high compliment of placing in my hands the whole
business of purchasing nitrates for the United States from
Chili. The Headquarters of the Inter-Allied Nitrate Commission were necessarily in London, and although the American Government was buying at least five times our requirements at this period, Mr. Baruch in a laconic telegram placed
American interests in my hands. I now became the Nitrate
King—the greatest there will ever be; and I reigned for nearly
a year, apparently with acceptance. I formed a small department under my personal direction to cope with this entirely

novel responsibility. At its head was a gifted young officer, Major Stomm, now lost to us, to whom I am deeply indebted. I used the potent influence which the control of British and American purchases gave me, not only to procure nitrates, but to persuade the Chilian Government to hand over the sixteen valuable German ships which had taken refuge in Valparaiso Harbour. Two or three times a week I sent telegrams as long as letters to Mr. Baruch explaining exactly what we were doing, and he helped me and supported me throughout. The correspondence and its developments were only interrupted by the conclusion of the War. I print the culminating telegram:—

Mr. Churchill to Mr. Baruch,

September 12, 1918.

Secret and Personal.

The disablement by sabotage of German ships interned in Chilian ports appears to have been the immediate response to our nitrate agreement with the Chilian Government. It reveals that the Germans regard this agreement as a blow against themselves. . . . I therefore look forward hopefully to the negotiations I now propose to begin about the 1919 purchases, throughout the course of which my endeavour will be to secure the use of the German ships. . . . I cannot of course tell whether with the limited means at our disposal these objectives can be secured, but I am sure they are the ones to make for. I hope you agree. Meanwhile the first thing to do is to press the Chilian Government to put guards on the ships. It should be pointed out that if the Germans sink these ships in the fairway of the ports, the Chilian Government may be prevented from carrying out its nitrate contract. British and American interests in the execution of this contract give us each a right to make representations in this sense and within these limits. The acts of sabotage already committed afford the Chilian Government ample grounds. The British Foreign office have at my request pressed the Chilian Minister in London strongly to have the ships guarded, and he has telegraphed accordingly to his Government. I hope you may find it possible through the

channels open to you to make similar representations. We
need not commit ourselves any further than this at the present time. Pray let me know if any of your ships are hung up
for want of nitrates. The Chilians have assured me they will
do everything in their power to secure immediate cargoes being available.

Very Private.

I am becoming embarrassed by the difficulty of getting a
definite answer from the American War Department as to
what help they want us to give them in their artillery programmes for next year. You will understand that it is very
difficult to keep my programmes in suspense for so long. I
do not know whether you can say a helpful word to accelerate
decision one way or the other, but if so I should be very grate-
ful. Many thanks for your friendly message about the nitrate
deal. I am so glad you approve of my negotiations.

When we met in Paris during the Peace Conference, I found
that Mr. Baruch apparently considered me an authority upon
the deeper technical aspects of the nitrate trade. He one day
asked me my advice upon an urgent and complicated question
concerning it. But reputations are easier lost than gained.
I thought I would let well alone, and disengaged myself with
suitable modesty.

Day after day Stettinius, Loucheur and I grappled with the
problem of the United States artillery. The American War
Department now aimed at placing in the field eighty divisions,
numerically equal in infantry to two hundred British or
French divisions, by the end of June, 1919. The rate at which
American troops were landing in France was already far ahead
of their munitions programme. They hoped to have forty-
eight divisions in France by the end of 1918. The transfor-
mation of their industry was still incomplete, and they could
only arm from American sources a fraction of the men they
were devoting to the struggle. Armies of eighty divisions required nearly 12,000 guns of various natures, with an unceasing flow of ammunition thereafter. Towards this the United

States could not count on supplying more than 600 medium and heavy guns and howitzers. They could however provide the material out of which the immense established gun plants of France could make 8,000, and those of Britain 3,000 pieces. By the adoption of a proportion of the British pattern, all the American and Canadian factories which we had hitherto used could be made immediately available for United States needs, both in guns and ammunition. The well-known disadvantages of a mixed armament lose much of their importance when armies are upon the giant scale, especially if each nature of gun is uniform throughout the national forces.

All was finally arranged, and the following is my report to the War Cabinet of the British share in these large transactions:—

SUPPLIES TO THE UNITED STATES ARMIES

To the War Cabinet.

September 25, 1918.

The United States in response to our appeals are sending men to Europe far in advance of their general munitions programme. Their shell programme is hopelessly in arrear [of these increased numbers]. Their gun programme is even worse. Not only in the main staples of equipment, but in a very large number of minor supplies, they will find themselves deficient. Unless therefore the arsenals of Great Britain and France can supply these deficiencies, the Americans cannot be expected to continue pouring in men, and the armies available for 1919 must be proportionately reduced. On the other hand, there is reason to believe that, working together, the French and British munition works can supply fully the needs of all the United States troops which can be brought by our maximum carrying capacity to Europe, and can supply them with good weapons and ample ammunition, provided only that the necessary raw materials are sent by America to be made up in our factories. No undue strain will be imposed upon our munition factories. The gun plants and the shell plants are running so smoothly now that, given raw material, they can easily meet their share of American needs. The processes of dilution and of releases of men will continue, in spite of this extra work, at a moderate rate. I am therefore pursuing the policy of doing everything possible to equip the United States armies, and offering every assistance in my power. I have agreed to supply them with more than 2,000 guns in 1919, and to make the ammunition for all these guns if they will send the raw materials. By this deal alone, considerably more than one hundred millions of British indebtedness to America will be extinguished. It seems to me indispensable that this process, to which we are deeply committed, should continue.

The longer we worked with the Americans, and the more interdependent our affairs became, the better grew our relations. In October we got rid of all sorts of rules prescribed in the early days of our association, and fell back on a 'gentleman's agreement' to help each other by every conceivable means, the sole test being the relative importance of particular services to the common cause.

To the War Cabinet.

October 3, 1918.

I have been approached by various officers of the American Expeditionary Force on the question of replacement from the United States of material used in supplies produced in this country for the American Army.

More than a year ago we insisted upon the policy of replacement for three reasons:—

(1) At a time when a number of officers were asking for quantities of goods, estimated on a basis which we could not test, we found it useful to insist that these officers should get an assurance of replacement from Washington as some sort of guarantee of urgency.

(2) At that time we were not certain to what extent our own orders would be squeezed out by the competition of the American programme.

(3) The Shipping Controller naturally insisted that we should claim an allocation of an equivalent American tonnage.

As regards (1), the urgency of requirements is now much more fully understood both by the American staff and by ourselves, and is examined by Inter-Allied organisations set up for the purpose.

As regards (2), we are still apprehensive about our supplies from the United States. But we are compelled to admit that during the last eighteen months we have never, in fact, been denied supplies which have been really urgent, and we must assume that the United States Government will continue to meet us in the same spirit. In fact, they do their utmost to help us, and in spite of our special counter-claims we are heavily in their debt.

As regards tonnage, the Shipping Controller is making bargains with the American Government on much broader lines than the exchange of tens of thousands of tons, and I understand he no longer wishes us to bargain ton for ton as before.

In these circumstances, I propose to accede to the wishes of the American Army, to waive the question of replacement of specific quantities of material for particular cessions, and to rely on the broad principle that we are to help each other to the utmost of our ability. I shall however keep a full account of the material used in the goods supplied to the United States, and shall naturally continue to put these figures before the United States representatives when discussing with them the allocation from the United States of bulk supplies to Great Britain. I am sure this is the wisest course to pursue, and the most likely to secure American assistance. *Nothing in the above proposals affects the question of money payments, which are all adjusted in the regular way.*[1]

I should be glad however to have the concurrence of the War Cabinet before definitely informing General Pershing that I am waiving our claim to specific replacement.

It is pleasing to revive these memories in years no longer terrible but sometimes bleak. No British Minister had, I believe, a greater volume of intricate daily business to conduct with United States representatives than I had during 1918. It is my duty to record the fact that no Ally could have given more resolute, understanding, and broadminded

[1] My subsequent italics.

co-operation than the Ministry of Munitions received from the War Industries Board of the United States. These sentiments were reciprocated. I enjoy the honour of being the only foreign member of their post-war Association, and with the King's permission I wear the United States Distinguished Service Medal presented me by General Pershing.

*   *   *   *   *

I have described the admirable behaviour of the munition workers during the crisis of the twenty-first of March. Misfortune and a sense of emergency seemed always to bring out their highest qualities. But once the situation at the front became easier, a wave of unrest swept across the factories. In the main this was born of overstrain; but beneath the surface, always ready to exploit any psychological reaction, lurked the pacifist and subversive elements of the labour world. In July a whole series of strikes broke out in the munition industries at centres as widely separated as Sheffield, Avonmouth, Oldham, Coventry, Gateshead, Farnham, Birmingham, Manchester, Hendon, Gainsborough, and Newport. Most of these disputes were composed, and many others prevented, by the ceaseless and skilful activities of the Munitions Labour Department under Sir Stephenson Kent. But Coventry proved intractable. We were confronted with a widespread cessation of work by the highly paid men engaged in the production of aeroplane engines, thus seriously endangering our programmes. After consulting the Prime Minister I decided to take the step from which we had hitherto always abstained of withdrawing from men who would not work, their munitions protection against being taken for the Army. In order that the case might be fully explained to the public and to the workers throughout the country, I assembled as was the custom on critical occasions in the war, the representatives of the Newspaper Proprietors' Association. Fifty or sixty gentlemen attended, covering virtually the entire Press.

I could see from their faces as I proceeded that they viewed the decision with concern, deepening in some quarters into consternation.　Despite their misgivings all undertook to sustain the national policy, and the Prime Minister continued resolute.　On July 16 I therefore issued the following notice which was displayed everywhere in Coventry.

July 16, 1918.

Owing to the scarcity of skilled labour in the country created by the needs of the Army and the grave emergency of the war, it became necessary some time ago to make sure that the skilled labour available was fairly shared among munition firms, and in some cases to place a limit on the number of skilled workers which particular employers or firms were entitled to engage.　If this had not been done, employers, instead of making reasonable efforts to economise skilled labour so that what we have might be used to the best public advantage, would have been led to scramble against each other for skilled men regardless of the national interest.　One firm would have been overcrowded with skilled men; another doing equally important war work would have been stopped for want of them.　The Defence of the Realm Act therefore gives power to the Government to limit the right of employers to engage skilled labour beyond their proper needs, and the use of this power was approved by the War Cabinet and announced on June 8th.

It is also the law that trade disputes in time of war shall be settled by arbitration without a stoppage of work.　But the strike which is threatened at Coventry is not a trade dispute.　It does not arise out of the ordinary relations of Capital and Labour.　It cannot be settled by arbitration.　It can only be regarded as an attempt to subvert and deflect the avowed policy of the State in time of national danger.

In consequence of this fact, the Minister of Munitions finds it necessary to state at the earliest moment that men who abandon their work in these circumstances will by that very act divest themselves of any protection against recruitment for the Army if they are liable to serve.　It is already hard that men between forty and fifty should be called up for the Army while younger men are left to earn high wages in the munitions factories. Only the fact that these men are absolutely needed at their work has induced the nation reluctantly to put up with what is from any other point of view unfair. It would indeed be wrong that a young man who is given special protection from recruiting to enable him to do work of great importance should refuse to do that work and yet that his protection should continue.

The Minister has therefore obtained the authority of the War Cabinet, not only to proceed with the utmost rigour of the law against all persons conspiring or inciting to such a cessation of work, but also to make it clear that the protection from military service of all or any men who cease work in these circumstances will be allowed to lapse immediately.

An anxious week-end intervened. On the Monday considerable numbers of men from the Seamen and Fireman's Union, many of whom had been submarined more than once, entered Coventry headed by Mr. Havelock Wilson and preceded by bands; and at the same time the organisation of the former Women's Suffrage Societies, under the fiery guidance of Miss Christabel Pankhurst, descended in a cloud of speakers, propagandists and canvassers. Patriotic meetings were held in all parts of the town. Under these varied pressures the strike collapsed, and by Tuesday night all Coventry was at work again.

* * * * *

From May onwards the Commander-in-Chief had assigned me regular quarters in the zone of his armies. I had a few rooms and facilities for a mess in an old French country-house amid wonderful avenues of trees near the village of Verchocq. I could reach this by aeroplane in two hours from Hendon, and so could upon occasions work at the Ministry of Munitions in the morning and follow the course of a great battle in the afternoon. I could come and go where I pleased on the front, and so far as it was possible without undue risk, could see all that there was to be seen. About one-fifth of my business lay at Headquarters or in Paris, where the Ministry of Munitions had large establishments. One way or another, either with General Tudor or with General Lipsett until he was killed, and also with Sir Alexander Godley, or with General Birdwood and the Australian Corps in which my brother was serving, or with Rawlinson's army, I managed to be present at almost every important battle during the rest of the war. Once I flew in a fighting plane between the lines while a considerable action was in progress below. But from the height of 7,000 feet to which we had to keep on account of the German artillery, there was nothing to see but the bursting shells of the barrages far below. It is impossible to see a modern battle. One is always either much too far or much too near.

Meanwhile the schemes and preparations for 1919 were moving steadily forward. Maeterlinck says the God of the bees is the future. At the Ministry of Munitions we were the bees of Hell, and we stored our hives with the pure essence of slaughter. It astonishes me to read in these after years the diabolical schemes for killing men on a vast scale by machinery or chemistry to which we passionately devoted ourselves. *'Les bons pères de famille sont capables de tout.'* We denied ourselves nothing that the laws of war with their German applications allowed. The Germans had installed cylinders of poison gas. We had followed them swiftly in these sinister experiments. In the end many more Germans died from British gas than British from German. In 1918 the enemy had far the larger supplies of the irritant mustard gas, but our outputs were broadening daily. Although the accidentally burned and blistered at the factories exceeded 100 per cent of the staff every three months, volunteers were never lacking.

The Mechanical Battle now took definite shape.